RICHARD L. MADISON

Raised from the

DEAD

A TRUE ACCOUNT

"With God nothing shall be impossible."
Luke 1:37

All Scripture quotations are taken from the King James Version (KJV) of the Bible.

OPERATION HEALING MINISTRY
INTERNATIONAL EVANGELIST RICHARD MADISON

Richard L. Madison
PO Box 205 • Oakman, Alabama 35579
(205) 622-5022 • www.rickmadison.org
ISBN-13: 978-0-942507-43-0
ISBN-13: 978-0-942507-50-8 (ebook)
Library of Congress Control Number: 2005933789

Publisher's Cataloging-in-Publication

(Provided by Quality Books, Inc.)

Madison, Richard L., 1961-
Raised from the dead : a true account / Richard L.
Madison. — 1st revision.
p. cm.

1. Madison, Richard L., 1961- 2. Healers—United
States—Biography. 3. Spiritual healing—United States.
4. Evangelists—United States—Biography. 5. Christian
biography—United States.   I. Title.

BT732.56.M33A3 2008   248.8'6'092
                              QBI08-600104

Published by **Deeper Revelation Books**
Revealing *"the deep things of God"* (1 Cor. 2:10)
PO Box 4260 | Cleveland, TN 37320 | 423-478-2843
www.deeperrevelationbooks.org

Wholesalers and retailers are invited to visit www.deeperrevelationbooks.org for information on our affiliated distributors.

Deeper Revelation Books assists Christian authors in publishing and distributing their books. Final responsibility for design, content, permissions, editorial accuracy and doctrinal views, either expressed or implied, belongs to the author.

"Jesus walked into that hospital room, and laid His hand on Rick Madison's head and healed him."

—Pat Robertson

"Fast living led to a dead end, but a new life began with an out-of-body experience."

—Ben Kinchlow

"Richard, you've had everything go wrong that could go wrong and...you are a living miracle. There must be a God in heaven, and He is truly watching over you."

—Dr. Kenneth Sharp
Attending Trauma Physician
Vanderbilt University Medical Center

References

Mike Shreve-International Evangelist, Publisher and Vice President of United Christian Church, Cleveland, TN—

"I believe Rick Madison would be a tremendous blessing to any church or ministry he works with. I believe God has especially graced him to build people's faith to expect healings and miracles. Every time I have heard him share his testimony, the anointing of God was always upon him to help God's people reach a new level of faith."

Sid Roth-Founder of the Messianic Vision radio program and the It's Supernatural television show, Brunswick, GA—

"Richard Madison was raised from the dead to preach and teach that Jesus is real and coming soon. Richard's book on healing is at another level."

Barry Lombard-Senior Pastor, Church of God, Jasper, AL—

"I have seen people blessed and healed as Richard fervently prays for everyone's needs. The lost are saved, the sick receive healing, and the oppressed are set free."

Perry Stone-International Evangelist, Author, Founder and Host of Manna Fest TV Show, Cleveland, TN—

"Rick Madison has one of the top three stories that I have ever heard in my life about people coming out of comas."

Contents

Foreword 9

Dedication 11

1. A Miracle When I Was Six Months Old 13

2. Death Stalks Me Once Again 21

3. My Out-of-Body Experience 31

4. More Miracles Follow 37

5 . Running Out of the Wheelchair 43

6. Bones Healed in Front of Doctors 53

7. The Day I Met an Angel 59

8. A Tumor Disappears Overnight 61

9. Dreams and Visions 63

10. Financial Miracles 83

11. My Kidneys Fail 91

12. What I Have Learned 107

13. Testimonies of Others 111

Prayer to be Born Again 119

About the Author 121

Audio and Books 122-128

Webster's Dictionary defines miracle as: 1. And extraordinary event manifesting divine intervention in human affairs. 2. A divinely natural phenomenon experienced humanly as the fulfillment of Spiritual Law.

Foreword

The Lord instructed me to write this book. He moved on me by His Spirit in a very personal way, and He is about to do the same for you! If you are not already a believer, this book will inspire you to become one. God's presence is so powerful, yet so peaceful. Just relax, and be prepared to feel the presence of God.

In 1986, I was pronounced DOA at Vanderbilt University Hospital. I was on a gurney being rolled to the morgue, as my family prayed for a miracle. After an out-of-body experience, and an encounter with God, I awoke out of a twenty-seven day coma.

Many people have gone from rags to riches in this world. Truly I am one of those people. I am spiritually rich. I am born again by the blood of Jesus Christ, and I have taken on His righteousness. I am a joint-heir with Christ! The apostle Paul wrote, *"And if children, then heirs; heirs of God, and joint-heirs with Christ"* (Romans 8:17). I can now say what Paul said in Philippians 4:19; *"But my God shall supply all* [my] *need according to his riches in glory by Christ Jesus."*

Allow this book of testimonies to draw you closer to the living God and His Holy Word, the Bible. You will notice that I give names and addresses in this book whenever possible—both of people who have received healings and miracles. I know that you will be amazed at my own story.

Many people say that miracles do not happen anymore, but I believe in miracles. I am a miracle! I was raised from my deathbed. I got up out of a wheelchair and walked. I am a living testimony of miracles. Why? Because of faith!

The author of Hebrews told us, *"Jesus Christ* [is] *the same yesterday, and to day, and for ever"* (Hebrews 13:8).

Remember, God does not change. If He worked miracles for people in times past, He will work the same things for people today and in the future.

He will move for you today. All you have to do is believe. Exercise your faith, which is given to you by God. In Romans 12:3 we are told, *"According as God hath dealt to every man the measure of faith."* You have been given faith by God. Use it! Now, right now, thank God for your miracle ahead of time.

Serving God is the most marvellous adventure I have ever experienced. We walk with God by faith, we are saved by faith, we are healed by faith, and we are filled with His Holy Spirit by faith. *"So then faith cometh by hearing, and hearing by the word of God"* (Romans 10:17). This book is about helping you to hear and receive from God.

I am a walking miracle, having been raised from the dead. But the greatest miracle is that I've been born-again— born of the Spirit and of water (John 3:5)! You can have this miracle of being born-again right now, and you don't have to go through the physical misery that I went through. Just ask and believe. Salvation, healing, and deliverance belongs to the people of God. Use this book to learn who you are in Christ, and about your inheritance.

Do as we are told in Romans 10:9; *"If thou shalt confess with thy mouth the Lord Jesus, and shall believe in thine heart that God hath raised him from the dead, thou shalt be saved."*

Read this book all the way through, and then share it with others. I have prayed that God would put this material in the hands of those who need to hear a word from Him.

—RICHARD L. MADISON

Dedication

This book is dedicated in loving memory of William Robert Graham—a man of honor, integrity and faithfulness to Jesus Christ and his family. Jesus is rewarding him abundantly.

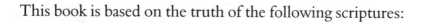

This book is based on the truth of the following scriptures:

"And Jesus looking upon them saith, with men it is impossible, but not with God: for with God all things are possible." (Mark 10:27)

"For with God nothing shall be impossible." (Luke 1:37)

"And these signs shall follow them that believe; in my name shall they cast out devils; they shall speak with new tongues; they shall take up serpents; and if they drink any deadly thing, it shall not hurt them; they shall lay hands on the sick, and they shall recover." (Mark 16:17-18)

A Miracle When I Was Six Months Old

O n May 10, 1961, I was a six-pound, seven-ounce baby boy, born to R. L. and Jewel Upton Madison. The birth took place in Jasper, Alabama, at People's Hospital.

Times were hard for many families in the sixties. Some had to travel to distant places to find work. My parents were raised in Fayette County and Walker County, Alabama, but hard times forced them to move north to find work. My family moved to Chicago, Illinois.

After we had gotten settled, and I was six months old, something happened that brought about the first miracle in my life. I fell off a couch, and my head hit the floor. I went into a coma. The doctors were unable to bring me out of the coma, and the likelihood of my survival could only be guessed from day to day. After the third day, the doctors said I would never regain consciousness. But after six days and six nights, praise God, I came out of the coma!

You see, my mother had continued to believe that God would raise me up. The doctors were amazed. With joy they gave the good report. I believe now, as I look back, that God had people praying and interceding on my behalf. As we are told in Romans 8:26-28,

> *Likewise the Spirit also helpeth our infirmities: for we know not what we should pray for as we ought: but the Spirit itself maketh intercession for us with groanings which cannot be uttered.*
> *And he that searcheth the hearts knoweth what is the mind of the Spirit, because he maketh intercession for the saints according to the will of God.*
> *And we know that all things work together for good to them that love God, to them who are the called according to his purpose.*

We see in these verses that God wants to accomplish three things. First of all, He wants to pray through us by His Spirit with groanings, or, with a prayer language. Secondly, He wants to accomplish His will, so that when the Spirit prays through us, He prays the will of God. God knows what we need before we do! According to what we read in John's third letter, it is God's will for us to be in health and prosper: *"Beloved, I wish above all things that thou mayest prosper and be in health, even as thy soul prospereth"* (3 John 1:2). We pray often for God to heal us, but, if we will let the Spirit pray through us, He will heal all our infirmities! Thirdly, God wants us to realize that all things work for our good if we love Him. He has a purpose for us.

I have said all of that to say this: God did not put me in a coma for my good; He brought me out of the coma for my good and His purpose! I believe God knew ahead of time that I would go into another coma again at age twenty-four. My family was able to look back and say, "God did it once before, He can do it again!

We must keep the right attitude about our difficulties and trials. We must not blame God foolishly. Jesus said in John 10:10, *"The thief cometh not, but for to steal, and to kill, and to destroy."* We read in James 1:17, *"Every good gift and every perfect gift is from above, and cometh down from the Father."* Sure, God corrects those whom He loves, but He does not inflict us with sicknesses, diseases, or comas in order to teach us something. If we stray from God and lose His peace, and live in sin, God will allow such things in our lives in order to teach us all He wants us to know.

God had a purpose in allowing two comas in my life, I have now prayed for sixteen people in comas, and fourteen have awakened! Six of them were brain dead.

Prayer Warriors

When we have been delivered from something, God will oftentimes use us to help others, who are in the same situation. Our testimony, and faith that came from seeing God move for us, will encourage others to have hope.

Although several of my family members were not believers at the time of my first coma, God used people from all over the world to pray for me through intercession. My grandmother was a believer in Jesus, and she called everyone she knew who would be able to pray for me. In turn, those people called other prayer warriors, and a large network of prayer was formed. Remember, if you love God or if He has a purpose for you, He will have people interceding for you whenever you are undergoing a trial. By the time of my second coma, more people in my family became believers, so I had even more people praying for me.

God responds to prayer. God answers prayer. James told us, *"Pray one for another, that ye may be healed"* (James 5:16). If we pray for someone who has the same need that we have, often God will deliver us. He wants us to pray for one another and to love one another. The Holy Spirit will place a burden on your heart to pray for someone, and God will bless or heal you. Ask God to reveal to you His purpose for your life.

Think back to all the incidents and accidents in which you could have been taken out of this life. If you are born again, God has put a hedge of protection around you and your family. The Bible talks about this hedge in the book of Job. Job feared God, avoided evil, and served God with sacrifices, and God had a hedge around Job and his family. Satan told God, *"Hast not thou made an hedge about him, and about his house?"* (Job 1:10).

In the Old Testament, offering sacrifices, as Job did, was part of being righteous before God. In the new covenant, Jesus has become our sacrifice. *"Christ, who through the eternal Spirit offered himself"* (Hebrews 9:14), has *"put away sin by the sacrifice of himself"* (verse 26). He is also our High Priest, our Hedge, our Older Brother. So, if Jesus is on our side, who can be against us and win (Romans 8:31). Remember, all things will work for your good if you will yield your life to Jesus and seek the kingdom of God with all your spirit, soul, and body.

Little Children Go to Heaven

I do believe that if I had died at the age of six months I would have gone to heaven. Many parents, after losing a child, have asked me if their child is in heaven. Even though all of us are born into a world of sin, each person grows and comes to a place called the age of accountability. Only God knows whether a child or a young person who passes away at an early age has reached the point of knowing right from wrong. If a child or young person dies before reaching that point, he or she automatically goes to heaven. Jesus provides the salvation that he or she needs. If you are a parent who has lost a child at a very young age, rest assured, for God takes care of His children.

James 4:14 tells us, *"For what is your life? It is even a vapour, that appeareth for a little time, and then vanisheth away."* This means that we ought to work for God now, while we can, while it is still day. This Scripture does not imply that we will disappear into thin air one day, never to be seen again. If a child or a born-again Christian dies, he or she is in the presence of Christ, as Paul described in 2 Corinthians 5:8: *"To be absent from the body, and to be present with the Lord."* If we endure to the end, we will again see our loved ones who are in heaven. Have faith in God and confidence in His Word!

Death Comes Close Again

There were several more times when I faced death as a child. When I was five years old, one of my great uncles lost his mind and tried to kill me and my grandmother. He drove into our front yard and got out of his car with a rifle in his hand. I was on the porch. I spoke to him. He aimed the rifle and began shooting.

The bullets hit the door that was near where I was standing, just inches from my head. I ran inside and hid under the bed, with fear gripping my mind and my body. My grandmother was shot four times and fell just inside the doorway. Later, my great uncle drove up the highway and killed himself.

My grandmother was at the point of death in the hospital, but the Lord raised her up. She fully recovered after this incident. She lived to be ninety-three years old and went home to Jesus in 2003. A brief testimony is given by Grandmother Upton in chapter thirteen.

Once again, God had protected me. Praise His name! I did not know then that His protective eye was on me. But I do now!

Another meeting I had with death happened when I was eight years old. I was playing hide-and-seek with my cousins in a public laundromat. I climbed into a large commercial dryer to hide. I left the glass door open far enough so that I could still get air.

Suddenly, the front door of the laundromat was thrown open, and a gang came in. A tall, long-haired man, about twenty years old, came over to the dryer where I was hiding. After he saw me, he shut the dryer door. He took some money out of his pocket and began to search for the correct change to start the machine.

As soon as I saw him, I panicked. I began to scream and cry. I knew what he was going to do. He held the door shut as he laughed, looking at me. I could see the devil in him. I tried to kick the door open, but he held it too tightly. I knew that if he found the right money and started the machine, I would probably die.

The girl who was with him began to beg him to let me out. Then she started to scream and fight with him to let me out. Finally, he opened the door. Then the gang left just as quickly as they had come in. I ran home to my mother, knowing I was now safe. Once again, God had protected me.

I don't ever want to forget God's benefits. Think of all the times God has saved you when you were in trouble.

Somehow you survived the trouble and came out a winner. You should continually thank God. Give Him the credit!

Once when I was a child living in Chicago, Illinois, I was playing with two friends in the basement. A man came in and pulled out a knife. He began to tell us he was going to kill us one by one. I managed to escape, and I ran and told my father what was happening. He called the police and then he scared the man off and rescued my two friends.

When I was 14 years old, a man broke into our home. He had a gun and decided to kidnap my mother. I jumped into the car beside my mother in the front seat as he started to leave. I believed I could help save my mother from harm. The police pulled us over about 20 miles later and rescued my mother and I. The Lord has surely kept His angels all around me since my birth. His mercy endureth forever!

Death Stalks Me Once Again

When I was six years old, my parents were divorced. After that, I did not live in one place very long. I lived with one parent or the other. I often went to live in the homes of different relatives. I traveled a lot, though not by my own choice. I did not know it then, but God was getting me accustomed to traveling. He knew I would need this experience later in my life.

Growing up in this manner has helped me to be a better evangelist. Traveling from place to place is now very natural to me. I have known no other way of life. Evangelists must enjoy traveling, or they will quickly become discouraged. An evangelist lives on the road. His ministry consists of traveling from church to church, wherever the Holy Spirit leads.

Before I graduated from high school, I lived in several states and went to seventeen different schools. I now consider it a miracle that I received a high school diploma. In the eleventh grade, I quit school. During the time I was out of school, I worked two jobs. But after a short time, I was ready to go back to school, and I earned my diploma.

I had studied heating and air-conditioning in vocational school while attending high school in Leeds, Alabama. My grades were good enough that I received a scholastic award when I graduated in 1980. I then went to work at the University of Alabama at Birmingham. I worked as a HVAC (heating, ventilation and air-conditioning) mechanic. I left that job after three years and moved to Nashville, Tennessee, where I worked as a technician for a couple of fast-food chains. In 1985 I began my own business as a maintenance company contractor. Soon I was making big money. I began to spend that money on alcohol, drugs, and riotous living.

I had attended church as a child, and I was saved when I was ten years old, but I never really understood everything I was told about God. I knew He loved me, but I did not know why He loved me. I had attended a Baptist church with some relatives and a Pentecostal church with others. I could tell the two churches were different, but I did not know why.

Even though I had lived my life mostly without God, my conscience bothered me when I was at parties and took drugs. My business was booming, but I had no real peace or happiness. In April of 1986, I almost overdosed on cocaine. I could sense a war going on for my soul. I remembered the name of Jesus from the times when I had attended church as a boy. I asked Jesus to help me. I asked Him to deliver me from drugs, if He had the power. I asked Jesus to change my life. I asked Him to give me a testimony. I survived the overdose, but I did not give up the alcohol. The very next week I was drinking again, but I steered clear of cocaine.

A Head-On Crash

That week I attended an all-night party. It was April 13, 1986. I was driving home around 6:45 A.M., and I went to sleep at the wheel. My Ford Ranger hit a brand-new Delta

88 Oldsmobile head-on! This happened near the airport in Nashville, Tennessee. The people who were in the car that I hit suffered broken bones and have recovered.

The Oldsmobile Delta 88 that I hit

The impact pushed the motor almost into the cab of my truck. I was in shock and unconscious. My chest had slammed into the steering wheel, causing it to fold backward. All the ribs in my chest were broken. One rib pushed through near my heart and punctured the aorta artery. My right lung was punctured and my spleen also. A vertebra in my neck was cracked. My left jaw, left hip, and right ankle were broken. Blood began to pour into my stomach. I was later told that the spleen holds two pints of blood as a reservoir in the human body.

The paramedics finally arrived. After working for some time, they freed me from my truck. I was then taken to Vanderbilt University Hospital. They have a top-rated trauma unit. By this time, most of my blood was in my stomach. I was still in shock, and the paramedics knew I was at the point of death. Nearly forty minutes had passed in which no oxygen reached my brain.

I was pronounced DOA (dead on arrival), but the main trauma doctor told me later that something told him to try to revive me. He then had me brought back to the O.R.

My 1984 Ford Ranger truck

My family was called in. Some of them lived in Tennessee, others lived in Alabama. My family was given no hope. I was considered brain-dead, since very little blood had been available to carry oxygen to my brain. Remember, forty minutes had passed by. Three liters of systolic solution were put into my veins intravenously.

A splenectomy was performed in order to remove my ruptured spleen. My aorta was sewn up. It later tore open and had to be sewn up again. A pocket of infection formed in my left side, causing a severe abscess. Tubes were placed in my nose to allow me to breathe. Later, a tracheal tube was put in my throat. Ventilating hoses were connected to this tube. My right eye had been knocked out of its socket. It was put back in place, but nerve damage had been done. My family was informed that, if I survived, a glass eye would be put in at a later date.

After the accident, I remained in a coma for twenty-seven days. My left leg was put in traction with a forty-pound weight until surgery could be performed. This was needed to keep the leg from getting shorter than the other leg. My situation looked hopeless. But I had some prayer warriors on my side. Praise God! Several prayer chains were

My truck from the driver's side

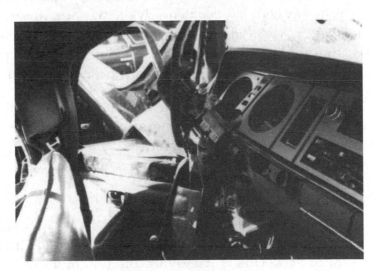

My truck from the passenger's side

called, including ones at *The 700 Club* and the Trinity
Broadcasting Network. They interceded on my behalf.
Many, many churches were praying.

My bones remained broken for twenty-five days. The
doctors did not think it necessary to repair them when it
seemed I probably would not pull through. I had so many
internal injuries that bones were secondary, anyway. I
received a total of 124 pints of blood. I caught hepatitis, blood
poisoning, double pneumonia and jaundice. Later, my liver
and kidneys stopped functioning.

The doctors called my family in to see me for the last
time on three different occasions. The third time, funeral
arrangements were advised. I had turned yellow and begun
to smell. My dad later told me that he had to hold his nose
the last time he came in to see me.

No medicine existed that could make my liver and
kidneys start working again. All the up-to-date medicines
and antibiotics were being administered. I was given
morphine every three hours to make sure my body was free
from pain. My body swelled to nearly the size of a fifty-five
gallon barrel! My head was almost the size of a basketball.
Every time the breathing machine pumped air into my lungs,
blood would come out of my eyes, ears, nose and mouth.

My mother spent every night at the hospital the entire
time I was there. She only left during the day one time. I
remained in the intensive care unit (ICU) for thirty-three
days. I was in the hospital a total of forty-nine days.

Broken Neck Healed

One of my uncles began to pray that God would heal
my broken neck. God spoke to him and told him that my
neck was healed. Praise God! He called my family at the

ICU waiting room to tell them that my neck was healed, and that he was standing on the Word of God. Praise His name!

Later, a CT-scan was taken to see where I was losing blood. Dye was put in my blood to find the leak. That's when they discovered that the aorta had torn loose again. This is also when they discovered the abscess in my side. Exploratory surgery was performed. The films revealed that the vertebra in my neck was healed.

The doctors removed the brace from my neck. Now I could be rolled and rotated on the bed. The abscess had been removed, and the aorta was again repaired. I was still considered brain-dead, but miracles were happening. God was answering prayers because people were believing.

I had eighteen tubes in my chest. Seventeen were for draining, and one was a feeding tube. I had no water in my mouth for over thirty days. But my God is merciful. I could have been left for dead, and I would have gone to hell, where I would never have received another drop of water.

Three people were believers in my family: my mother, my aunt Audra, and my uncle Joe. When everyone else was arguing about where to bury me, these three had decided to raise the dead. These three believers came in and anointed me with oil and prayed the prayer of faith. The Scripture tells us to do this:

> *Is any sick among you? let him call for the elders of the church; and let them pray over him, anointing him with oil in the name of the Lord:*
> *And the prayer of faith shall save the sick, and the Lord shall raise him up; and if he have committed sins, they shall be forgiven him.*
> (James 5:14-15)

Some of my family and friends had never seen a miracle. Two of my friends became born-again believers as they began to pray for me. Others could not understand how to believe to bring about a miracle, because they were not born-again. They had no personal relationship with Jesus.

As I lay there, stinking and turning yellow, and organs not functioning, the doctors advised the family to make funeral arrangements again and explained that the machines would be disconnected. The three believers continued to intercede in the prayer room. My mother told me later that my body had become as hard as a rock.

A man named Rodney Lindsey came 200 miles to pray for me. After anointing me with oil, and praying the prayer of faith, he told my family what the Lord revealed to him. Brother Lindsey said, "I know you were told to make funeral arrangements. The Holy Spirit told me Richard will be raised up, and he will preach God's Word all over the world."

Brother Lindsey then held up his Bible, and said, "Thus saith the Lord God, I will perform this miracle before your eyes." My family stood there looking at Brother Lindsey in total amazement.

VANDERBILT UNIVERSITY MEDICAL
DISCHARGE SUMMARY
VANDERBILT UNIVERSITY HOSPITAL

ATTENDING PHYSICIAN

Kenneth Sharp, MD
MCN

PATIENT: MADISON, Richard
ADMITTED: 4/13/86
UNIT NO. 91 73 73
DISCHARGED: 5/31/86

DISCHARGE DIAGNOSIS: (1) Multiple trauma
secondary to motor vehicle accident.

SECONDARY DIAGNOSIS: Ruptured thoracic aorta;
Splenic rupture; Left acetabulum fracture; Right
trimalleolar ankle fracture; Left subphrenic abscess.

OPERATIONS: (1) Exploratory laparotomy,
splenectomy, tube gastrostomy, left chest tube
insertion, left subclavian central venous pressure line
insertion on 4/13/86. (2) Repair of ruptured thoracic
on 4/13/86. (3) Exploratory thoracotomy with
control of hemorrhage on 4/14/86. (4) Open
reduction, internal fixation of right trimalleolar
fracture on 5/8/86. (5) Open reduction and internal
fixation of left acetabular fracture on 5/8/86. (6)
Drainage of left subphrenic abscess on 4/28/86. (7)
Open reduction and internal fixation of mandibular
fracture on 5/8/86.

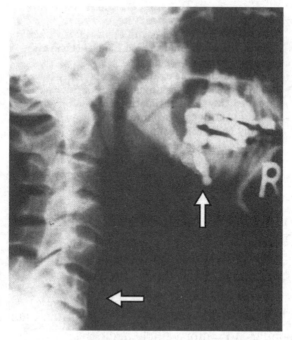

X-ray of C-5 vertebra and plate in jaw

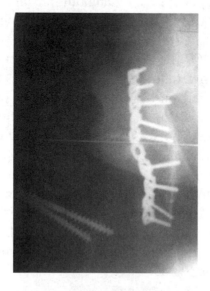

X-ray of hip

My Out-of-Body Experience

At one point all of my family decided to go to the first floor of the hospital to the prayer chapel. It must have been at this time that my spirit left my body. My body was lifeless in the ICU department. No brain activity was present. Twenty-seven days had passed since the accident. Two days earlier, the bones in my hip, my ankle, and my jaw had been reconstructed. When my hip was reconstructed, a steel plate with nine screws and two pins was put in its place. Three bones had been removed from my right ankle, and a steel rod and nine screws had been put in. A steel plate and two screws had been placed in my jaw. My mouth would be wired shut for seven weeks.

The bones were repaired because it seemed as though I might recover, and the doctors could wait no longer for my body to get stronger. But then, my liver and kidneys stopped, and I was going out into eternity.

My spirit left my body, and I saw myself walk down hallways, passing people. I walked into what I thought was a church. I saw my family and friends. I heard them praying for me and calling on the name of Jesus. I could see the red carpet and several pews. I could see everyone so clearly, but nobody could see me. Later on, I found out this was the prayer chapel at the hospital. I sat down and spoke to my mother, but she did not hear me.

The apostle Paul had what was probably an out-of-body experience, and he spoke about it in 2 Corinthians 12:2-4:

> *I knew a man in Christ above fourteen years ago, (whether in the body, I cannot tell; or whether out of the body, I cannot tell: God knoweth;) such an one caught up to the third heaven.*
> *And I knew such a man, (whether in the body, or out of the body, I cannot tell: God knoweth;)*
> *How that he was caught up into paradise, and heard unspeakable words, which it is not lawful for a man to utter.*

Paul could hear and see during this experience. He could not have made this happen by any of his own efforts, but it was God who allowed Paul to come into His presence.

In the same book, Paul further told us,

> *Therefore we are always confident, knowing that, whilst we are at home in the body, we are absent from the Lord:*
> *(For we walk by faith, not by sight:)*
> *We are confident, I say, and willing rather to be absent from the body, and to be present with the Lord.*
> (2 Corinthians 5:6-8)

I could not have caused myself to have this out-of-body experience. But God allowed this to happen to give me one more chance to call on His holy name. Many out-of-body experiences happens when one is near-death. I did not see a white light, nor did I pass through a tunnel as others have described. I went to a chapel where people were praying. When I realized that no one could see me, I knew something was wrong. I did not know of the accident, nor did I know I had left my body.

As I heard and watched my mother pray, I decided to do the same. I looked up toward the ceiling and said, "Jesus, if You are real, now is the time to come on the scene and help me." Wow! I felt a huge hand cover the top of my head, and I realized it had to be Jesus. No one else could hear me or see me.

I Heard His Voice

I heard His voice even as the apostle John did in the book of Revelation. It seemed like the sound of many waves crashing on the shore. Jesus said, "I am Jesus, and I will give you one more chance to serve Me. Go and tell My people that I am real and I still perform miracles. I still save, heal, and deliver, and I am coming soon." I pushed up against that huge hand. I tried to look around at Him, but He would not let me.

Raised from the Dead

Immediately, I left the prayer chapel and went back into my body. I went back in a flash, much quicker than I had left. All of a sudden I sat up in bed. I was still in the ICU. I came out of the coma instantly! Praise the Lord!

The nurse was at the foot of my bed. I reached for her, but I could not straighten my arms all the way. The ligaments had contracted in my body. When she saw me sitting up, reaching for her, she screamed. Just think, one minute the doctors wanted to pull the plug, the next minute I'm awake! After the nurse screamed, it seemed to me that she jumped up and said, "You're awake; you're alive!" I was trying to speak, but because of the tracheal tube, I couldn't make a sound.

The Gospels tell us the story of another man who was raised from the dead. His name was Lazarus. Lazarus had been dead for four days by the time Jesus got to where his body was, but Jesus said, *"Whosoever...believeth in me shall never die"* (John 11:26).

We know that our flesh will return to the dust unless Jesus returns for us first—in which case we will be changed, and mortality will clothe itself with immortality.

> *In a moment, in the twinkling of an eye, at the last trump: for the trumpet shall sound, and the dead shall be raised incorruptible, and we shall be changed.*
> *For this corruptible must put on incorruption, and this mortal must put on immortality.*
> (1 Corinthians 15:52-53)

Our spirit man is who we really are, and when we are born again, we know that we will live forever with Jesus in our new bodies.

Family Informed of the Miracle

The nurse handed me a piece of paper and a pen, and I wrote, "Is there a church here?" I had a hard time writing because my muscles had atrophied and my ligaments had tightened so much. But the nurse read what I had written, and she said, "You're at Vanderbilt University Hospital. You've been in a car wreck. But you're going to be okay now."

I wrote that the church I was asking about had red carpet and several pews. She read it and said, "You must be talking about the prayer chapel on the first floor." She added, "I don't remember what it looks like, it's been so long since I've been there."

I wrote, "My family is there praying for me. I know what it looks like. I just came from there!" She was amazed.

She asked another nurse to take my vital signs while she went to the first floor. My mother told me later that a nurse came into the prayer chapel and asked if they had a relative named Richard Madison. My mother told her that I was her son and that they were praying for me. Mother later told me that the nurse said, "You must be praying to the real God, because your son is sitting up and is doing much better!"

Normally, only two visitors were allowed into my room every four hours. Although it wasn't the scheduled visiting time, this was a special occasion. My mom and my aunt were allowed to come into my ICU room. They were holding each other's arms as they walked in. I saw their knees buckle, and they said, "I can't believe it! God has really done it! We were praying for it, and now we see it for ourselves! Praise the name of the Lord! Thank you, Jesus!"

Thank God for believers! Once again, I refer to Mark 16:17-18:

> *And these signs shall follow them that believe; In my name shall they cast out devils; they shall speak with new tongues;*
> *...they shall lay hands on the sick, and they shall recover.*

.

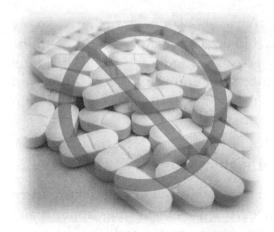

More Miracles Follow

The doctors gathered around my bedside, speaking medical language. I lay there staring at them as they stared at me. As the doctors repeatedly tried to give me credit for being alive, I pointed toward heaven. Finally, I wrote "Jesus" on a piece of paper and shook it at them. Then one of the doctors said, "Yes, Jesus has to be the reason that he's alive."

I was alive. Jesus had touched my brain, and I had no brain damage any more. But I was not out of the woods yet. My jaw, which had been repaired two days earlier, had become infected. The oral surgeon lanced my gums and removed a pocket of infection. My gums had to be repacked with new gauze every morning. They would not use any anesthetic to numb my gums. The pain was severe.

I had awakened from the coma on my birthday. I had turned twenty-five. When I thought about it, I knew that my life was just beginning. I began to look at myself in the mirror. I had a huge knot on my jaw. The doctor told me that it was scar tissue and that it would dissolve in six to eight months.

I communicated on notebook paper for about two more weeks. At first I was told that I would have to live with the tracheal tube in my throat. But, praise God, Jesus set me free! The tracheal tube was removed from my throat on May 21, 1986. And the hole in my throat began to heal on its own, without stitches!

Many Ministers Came to Pray

I was moved to the semi-trauma room after thirty-three days in the ICU department. During this time, many ministers had come by to pray for me, and I had begun to learn how to pray by listening to them. One day I placed my hand on the knot of scar tissue that was on my neck, and I asked the Lord to remove it by morning. I found out that God knows our very thoughts, because I could not speak out loud with the tracheotomy in my neck.

God does not have to hear our voices to hear our prayers. First Chronicles 28:9 tells us, *"The Lord searcheth all hearts, and understandeth all the imaginations of the thoughts."* If God knows our hearts and can hear our thoughts, then we don't ever have to speak out loud to receive. God still hears the prayers of people who cannot speak!

The next morning, the oral surgeon's assistant came in to change the gauze, and I grabbed his hand and put it on my jaw and neck, where the knot had been. I had not checked to see if it had disappeared, but I knew it would be gone. Immediately, the doctor said, "What happened to the knot? The knot is gone!" I pointed up and smiled. He knew I was referring to Jesus. He replied, "This is a miracle before my own eyes! I would not have believed it if I had not seen it with my own eyes!"

A man named Thomas, a follower of Jesus, did not believe that Jesus had risen from the dead until he put his fingers in the holes of Jesus' hands, where the nails had been. Then he said that he believed. Jesus told Thomas, *"Blessed are they that have not seen, and yet believed"* (John 20:29).

If we believe that Jesus died for us and rose again, and if we keep His commandments, then we are blessed, even though we have not seen Him. We can be healed of sickness and disease if we believe what Peter told us about Christ in 1 Peter 2:24:

> **Who his own self bare our sins in his own body on the tree, that we, being dead to sins, should live unto righteousness: by whose stripes ye were healed.**

I was being fed by a tube that had been surgically placed into my intestine. I began to pray that God would make a way for me to drink some liquids. No water had been given to me by mouth for about five weeks. My mouth was as dry as cotton! I began to throw up the baby formula that was being fed to me through the tube. The doctors decided to put me on high calorie milk shakes. I began drinking through a straw. God had answered me again! I continued drinking through a straw for about seven weeks.

I will never take so much for granted again as long as I live. Just drinking water out of a glass or saying hello on the telephone or going to the bathroom without a bedpan—all of these things are such a blessing to me.

Delivered from Morphine Instantly

I had been given high doses of morphine for thirty-five days, every three hours. I was told that this made me addicted to the drug. But the doctors said that I would gradually be weaned off the morphine. The main trauma doctor, Dr. Kenneth Sharp, said I would be switched to seventy-five milligrams of Demerol, then to fifty milligrams, and then to twenty-five. After that, I would start taking Percodan. From there, I would go from Tylenol 4, to Tylenol 3, to Tylenol 2, to Tylenol 1. Dr. Sharp said to me, "Hopefully, by then you will have no withdrawal symptoms."

I listened to him, but I began to believe that God had taken over my thoughts. Suddenly I wrote on a piece of paper that Jesus had raised me up from the dead and He would not allow me to be addicted to any medicine. He read this, raised his eyebrows, and said with a grin, "You really believe this, don't you?" I nodded my head yes. He said, "Well, we'll see what happens."

The orders were written on my charts to change my medicine. When the nurse came in to administer the first dose, I stopped her. I wrote, "It is not needed." She consented but then told me that I should call the nurses' station and tell them if I needed it.

My family was with me all this time. They took turns staying in my room. They really stuck by my side, helping me with every request. They watched as five days went by without me receiving any medication. On the fifth afternoon, Dr. Sharp came into the room with my charts in his hand. He pulled up a chair, sat down, and just looked at me for a while without saying a word.

Then he said, "Richard, I see on your charts here that you have refused your medication for the past five days. How are you?" I gave the "okay" sign with my hand. Then the doctor said, "Did you know I pronounced you DOA when you were rushed here? I know your mind is now okay, and your neck is no longer broken. You received a lot of blood and acquired many infections, which are now fading away. But Richard, I have never in my medical career seen anybody come off the amount of morphine that you have had, cold turkey! Truly there is a God in heaven, and He's watching over you!" While he was saying this, he stood up and pointed up. Several doctors looked in, and shook their heads in amazement.

I Could Speak and Praise the Lord

The doctors had taken the large tube out of my neck and had replaced it with a smaller one. I could place my finger over the tube at my throat and speak fairly well. When Dr. Sharp said I could go home, I raised one of my hands and began to cry. By closing the opening at my throat with my other hand, I started to thank God for being so merciful to me.

I really began to see what had happened to me by the miracle of God. He had freed me from all addictions—drugs, alcohol and nicotine! Here I was, in a place where people wanted to give me drugs, and I did not want any.

Truly, God had worked a miracle in me. Before the accident, I had spent a lot of money on drugs. And now I had been delivered from drugs without rehabilitation or counseling. When you are born-again, *"old things are passed away; behold, all things are become new"* (2 Corinthians 5:17).

The next day I asked the doctor how I could go home when I could not even walk. He told me I might never walk again, since my bones had been broken for twenty-five days and both sides of my lower extremities had been broken. He told me that if my ankle and hip had been broken on the same side, I could have walked on crutches. I was devastated. He said that the sciatic nerve in my left hip had been accidentally severed; that was why a splint had been placed on my left leg. I knew I didn't have any feeling in my left leg. I also had a cast on my right leg.

I could not imagine never walking again. I was told the sciatic nerve would grow back together in eight to ten months, and the feeling would begin to come back. I was told that I was lucky to be alive, because only about one out of a hundred thousand people live after experiencing a tear in the aorta and a ruptured spleen. Another doctor said I was one in a million. I continually thanked the hospital personnel, but I was giving the credit to Jesus.

They rigged a hoist to lift me up off the bed, and after they swung me around, they lowered me into a wheelchair. I was then wheeled outside for the first time since the accident. I had to put on sunglasses to protect my eyes, but even then the brightness still hurt. I felt as if I had been in a dungeon for years and was finally allowed to come to the surface.

I was told that I could go home on May 31, 1986. In six weeks, I would return for a follow-up examination. The feeding tube would be left in my stomach until the next visit. I had many scars on my chest and stomach, and much of the feeling was gone from those areas. At one point in time, I had nearly four hundred staples, which were used instead of stitches to hold the surgical areas closed. These staples were literally holding my body together!

Running Out of the Wheelchair

After forty-nine days in the hospital, I went home with my mother. She lived in Birmingham, Alabama. The two-hundred-mile trip from Nashville to Birmingham was a nightmare for me. I had such a fear of getting into an automobile again.

In order to travel to Birmingham, I had to lie down in the back of a van. I could see the traffic very well, and just seeing the traffic coming toward me sent pain up and down my body. But I began to pray, and the Lord removed the fear. If I had known the Scripture at the time, I would have repeated, *"For God hath not given us the spirit of fear; but of power, and of love, and of a sound mind"* (2 Timothy 1:7).

My mother had a hospital bed at her home, and I needed this to raise my head and legs. My left leg, which had a broken hip and severed sciatic nerve, began to hurt and ache often. I stayed with my mother for four weeks. She took very good care of me—as well as any mother ever took care of a child.

One day my aunt and uncle from Oakman, Alabama, came to see my mother and me. They asked me if I would like to visit them at their home for a while. I thought it might be good for both my mother and me. It would let her go back to work, and it would give me a change of scenery. So it was arranged.

I did not know it at the time, but I found out later that my aunt and uncle went to church five times a week. They went to services at a Church of God Fellowship on Sunday morning and Sunday night, then again on Tuesday night and Thursday night. On Wednesday nights they attended services at a fired-up Freewill Baptist Church. I knew Jesus was real by now for sure, but I did not think He would want me to go to church all the time!

At that time in my life, I thought I did not want this. But, to my surprise, the more I was carried to church, the more I wanted to go! The Word of God began to enlighten my understanding. I began to learn about God and what He required of me. I learned how much He loved me, and how I could be used by Him. You see, the more I heard the Word preached, the more my faith grew. Praise God! *"So then faith cometh by hearing, and hearing by the word of God"* (Romans 10:17).

Anointing with Oil

People anointed me with oil at almost every service, as James said to do:

> *Is any sick among you? let him call for the elders of the church; and let them pray over him, anointing him with oil in the name of the Lord:*
> *And the prayer of faith shall save the sick, and the Lord shall raise him up; and if he have committed sins, they shall be forgiven him.*
> (James 5:14-15)

They laid hands on me and prophesied over me. They told me that I would walk again and that I would preach the Gospel of Jesus Christ. I could hardly believe it. Yet, after going to church five times a week for four weeks, I realized I had the faith to believe that God could do anything. I found out that Jesus could do anything, and I began to believe that I could do all things through Jesus Christ. *"I can do all things through Christ which strengtheneth me"* (Philippians 4:13).

I was probably anointed with enough oil in that four-week period to grease an eighteen wheel truck. But it was worth every minute of it. I quoted the Scripture often that says, *"Jesus Christ* [is] *the same yesterday, and to day, and for ever"* (Hebrews 13:8). I knew that if anyone changed, it would have to be me, because Jesus, or the Word, can never change. I could feel a change coming over me. I realized I was in the presence of people who continually sought God, and it made me seek Him, too.

I began to read the Scriptures and put myself in the passages where others had been healed. When the centurion asked Jesus to heal his servant, Jesus said, *"I will come and heal him"* (Matthew 8:7). Because of verses like the following, I knew that God wanted to heal me and had sent His Word to heal me: *"He sent his word, and healed them, and delivered them from their destructions"* (Psalm 107:20).

I realized that God has given power to me, as it says in Matthew 9:8: *"But when the multitudes saw it, they marvelled, and glorified God, which had given such power unto men."* I read Mark's gospel, in which a man who could not move or walk was instructed by Jesus to arise and walk. Read this passage for yourself:

> **And they come unto him, bringing one sick of the palsy, which was borne of four.**

And when they could not come nigh unto him for the press, they uncovered the roof where he was: and when they had broken it up, they let down the bed wherein the sick of the palsy lay.

When Jesus saw their faith, he said unto the sick of the palsy, Son, thy sins be forgiven thee.

But there was certain of the scribes sitting there, and reasoning in their hearts,

Why doth this man thus speak blasphemies? who can forgive sins but God only?

And immediately when Jesus perceived in his spirit that they so reasoned within themselves, he said unto them, Why reason ye these things in your hearts?

Whether is it easier to say to the sick of the palsy, Thy sins be forgiven thee; or to say, Arise, and take up thy bed, and walk?

But that ye may know that the Son of man hath power on earth to forgive sins, (he saith to the sick of the palsy,)

I say unto thee, Arise, and take up thy bed, and go thy way into thine house.

And immediately he arose, took up the bed, and went forth before them all; insomuch that they were all amazed, and glorified God...

(Mark 2:3-12)

In John 5:5-9, Jesus told a man to take up his bed and walk, and the man did.

And a certain man was there, which had an infirmity thirty and eight years.

When Jesus saw him lie, and knew that

he had been now a long time in that case, he
saith unto him, Wilt thou be made whole?

The impotent man answered him, Sir,
I have no man, when the water is troubled,
to put me into the pool: but while I am
coming, another steppeth down before me.

Jesus saith unto him, Rise, take up thy
bed, and walk.

And immediately the man was made
whole, and took up his bed, and walked...

(John 5:5-9)

One minute he was lying on a cot, and the next minute the cot was on his shoulders, and he was running around.

I wanted to walk. I was tired of people having to bathe me and change my clothes and push me around in a wheelchair.

Mix Faith with Action

One day I said, "If Jesus is the same yesterday, today, and forever, then I am ready to be healed." I was sitting in the wheelchair and praying. I was saying everything I needed to say, but I had to mix faith and action with the Word. As James said, *"Even so faith, if it hath not works, is dead, being alone"* (James 2:17).

I was alone in the living room of my aunt and uncle's home. I raised my hands and prayed, "Lord, if You will just put feeling back in my legs, I will rise up and walk. I know You can put feeling in my legs." The doctors had told me not to put any weight on my lower extremities, or I would break the bones again.

All of a sudden, the Lord showed me a picture of some people toward whom I had hatred in my heart. I really did not know I had carried so much hatred toward them, but God knew I had. I said, "Lord, what are You showing me?"

The Lord said, "Call them, and tell them that you love them and forgive them, and that you want them to forgive you. You want to be healed, but I want you to forgive first!"

James 5:16 tells us, *"Confess your faults one to another, and pray one for another, that ye may be healed...."* And Mark 11:26 tells us, *"But if ye do not forgive, neither will your Father which is in heaven forgive your trespasses."* I said, "Lord, do I really have to call them? You know how badly they hurt me." The Lord said, "Do you want to walk again?" Then I knew what He was saying, and He did not have to say it twice!

Forgiveness

I thought about this for a while. I guess I was trying to figure out if it really was God or not. Jesus said, *"My sheep hear my voice, and I know them, and they follow me"* (John 10:27). As I thought about it, I realized it could not be the devil; he only comes *"to steal, and to kill, and to destroy,"* as we are told in John 10:10. And the devil would never tell someone to forgive.

So I made the long distance calls to the individuals. I told them that I had forgiven them and asked them to forgive me. I felt the anointing of the Holy Spirit come down on me, and I knew I was being healed. I said, "Okay, Lord, I've done what You wanted, and I feel different. I really do! So go ahead and put the feeling in my legs." Jesus spoke back to me, and this time it was like an audible voice. He said, "Rise and walk." It was a whisper that seemed to echo throughout the room.

I had just read a book by Kenneth Hagin called *Seven Things You Should Know About Divine Healing.* I knew that

"God is no respecter of persons" (Acts 10:34), which means if He helped Brother Hagin to walk, then He would help me to walk. I said, "I can't rise and walk, Lord. I don't have any feeling in my legs yet."

He answered, "You do not walk by feeling; you walk by faith."

"But how do I walk by faith?" I asked.

Jesus replied, "You just stand up and walk. It is not hard. Man has tried to make healing difficult by putting limits and doctrines on it, but I made it so simple. Just believe; accept your healing and walk."

I said, "Okay, Lord, here I go."

In the Name of Jesus, I Walked

I locked the wheels on the wheelchair. It had been eight full weeks since I had left the hospital, ten weeks since my bones had been reconstructed. As I put action to my words and mixed my faith with the Word of God, I stood on my feet.

My aunt and uncle were outside in the garden. Nobody was present to see this miracle happening. I always thought I would be at church and someone would say, "In the name of Jesus, arise and walk."

As I stood there on legs I could not feel, I thought I had better sit back down. I did not want to push my luck. Now I realize I am not lucky, but I am blessed. As often as we need a touch from God, He is always there.

As I started to sit down, I lost my balance. I started leaning forward. I said, "Oh, Lord, catch me; I'm falling!"

The devil said, "Yeah, you've gone and done it now. You've messed up big-time now." But I could feel the hand of God in that living room. There was a sofa bed there that had been pulled out for me to sleep on. Jesus said, "Trust Me." All of a sudden, I actually started running! My legs felt as if they were turning over, and I ran right around the bed. I was running before I walked! Praise God!

I suppose I looked funny, running across the room on numb legs, my arms stretched out, dodging furniture. I could not stop myself until I got to the doorway on the other side of the living room. I pondered how God had kept me up, how He had kept my legs moving, not letting me fall or break any bones. I started to cry, realizing I was not confined to a wheelchair for the rest of my life. I started seeing myself, as in a vision, doing such things as changing my own clothes and getting into a shower. I said, "Lord I'll never doubt You again; You are a miracle worker!"

"Trust Me"

Then I looked around and realized I was about twenty-five feet from my wheelchair and my bed. I said, "Oh, Lord, just get me back across the room without falling!" Once again, Jesus said, "Trust Me." I knew I had to lean forward and let go of the door jambs. I heard the voice of the Devil again. He told me I'd fall, that God wasn't with me. But I trusted the voice of God. I let go and leaned forward and began to run again. I grabbed the wheelchair. It swung around, and I sat down. I raised my hands and began praising the name of the Lord.

Later on, Jesus revealed to me that this is exactly what His people must do in order to walk with Him more closely. His people need to let go of some things, lean forward, and trust Him to help them walk. Holding on to the things of the world will make us lean toward the world, not toward Him. No matter how many times you have been put down or ridiculed, no matter how often you may have fallen, keep leaning on Him. Then you will not only walk, but you will run, too!

I heard my aunt and uncle come into the house. I thought about getting back up and showing them what Jesus had done. The Devil's voice came again, telling me I did not have the faith to try again. But the Word of God came back to me. In my mind I heard the words of Romans 12:3, telling me that I had been given a measure of faith: *"God hath dealt to every man the measure of faith."* And Matthew 17:20 flashed into my mind, saying:

> **And Jesus said unto them, Because of your unbelief: for verily I say unto you, If ye have faith as a grain of mustard seed, ye shall say unto this mountain, Remove hence to yonder place; and it shall remove; and nothing shall be impossible unto you.**

I figured that a measure of faith had to be more than the faith of the mustard seed. We actually have more faith than we need. All we have to do is exercise that faith.

I have found out that if we think Jesus is speaking to us, the word that we receive must line up with the Word of God. Praise God for His Word! The Word of God puts power in our words. Mark 11:23 says;

> **...That whosoever shall say unto this mountain, Be thou removed, and be thou cast into the sea; and shall not doubt in his heart, but shall believe that those things which he saith shall come to pass; he shall have whatsoever he saith.**

I said with my own lips that I would rise up and walk in the name of Jesus, and I did. I said I would preach the Gospel, and I do. I said I would testify of the healing power of God and how He saves and how He delivers today, and I have.

I Ran to my Aunt

As my aunt and uncle walked into the kitchen, I asked Jesus to let me stand and walk, or run, once again. I stood up and leaned forward, and my legs began to move. My upper body caused my lower body to follow. I ran right into the arms of my aunt. She screamed for my uncle to get a chair. She said to me, "Lord God, child, what are you doing? You're going to break every bone in your body!" I began to swing my arms to push her away.

By then, both of them were trying to push me down in a chair. I said, "I'm okay!"

They stepped back and looked at me so puzzled. I told them, "Jesus is healing me. You have been praying for me to walk, but instead God has allowed me to run!"

My aunt said, "Well, I can't believe it! But look at him, Joe, he's up on those legs! It just seems to be too soon."

I said, "You prayed the prayer of faith, and it worked. Now believe it." We began to praise the Lord for all of His benefits.

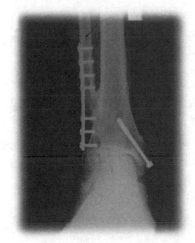

Bones Healed in Front of Doctors

I had lost fifty-two pounds since the time of the accident. This weight loss probably helped me in my early walking. After nine weeks, the steel wires were removed from my jaws. There were twenty of them. The doctors gave me nothing for the pain as they yanked out the wires. I cried and bled, but I endured it.

They said that my jaw was out of line. I prayed that God would line it back up, and He did. He has a way of lining things up. Each time the Lord healed me, He taught me something about healing, *"for to one is given by the Spirit...the gifts of healing"* (1 Corinthians 12:8-9).

I did not immediately start walking as I had done before the accident. I had to have some help. I used a walker at first in order to help me get my balance back. I still wanted to run anytime I walked somewhere. I had to grab somebody or something to stop myself from running. After using the walker for about a week, I began using a cane. I was walking better with each step. My leg began to get some of the feeling back in it. I believe I was healed through the gifts of healing when I walked out of the wheelchair for the first time, because the healing was gradual.

Pretty soon I began to feel so good that I tried to drive my own car, a Datsun 280Z. God had really moved on my behalf, so that I would not be afraid, and at the same time I would be a good driver. I had to improvise certain driving functions. With one of my hands, I would pick up my left leg to place my foot on the clutch, so that I could shift gears, since my car was a four-speed stick shift. My family and my friends were amazed that I could drive a four-speed car just four months after the accident.

Walking and driving were works of faith healing; they took time and came in stages, whereas a miracle happens instantaneously. Recall the miracles that occurred when I was in the hospital: I had no brain damage even though no blood or oxygen had reached my brain during a forty-minute period of time; I sat up, completely alert after being in a coma for twenty-seven days; the scar tissue knot disappeared from the side of my face; and my broken neck was healed. All these things were miracles. They happened in a flash!

In Matthew 9, we can see where Jesus performed miracles. In the following passages, Jesus raised a girl from the dead.

> *And when Jesus came into the ruler's house, and saw the minstrels and the people making a noise,*
> *He said unto them, Give place: for the maid is not dead, but sleepeth. And they laughed him to scorn.*
> *But when the people were put forth, he went in, and took her by the hand, and the maid arose.*
> (Matthew 9:23-25)

He also opened the eyes of two blind men:

> *And when Jesus departed thence, two blind men followed him, crying, and saying, Thou son of David, have mercy on us.*
>
> *And when he was come into the house, the blind men came to him: and Jesus saith unto them, Believe ye that I am able to do this? They said unto him, Yea, Lord.*
>
> *Then touched he their eyes, saying, According to your faith be it unto you.*
>
> *And their eyes were opened; and Jesus straitly charged them, saying, See that no man know it.*
>
> (Matthew 9:27-30)

These were miracles; they happened immediately. When a woman who had a bleeding for twelve years touched the hem of Jesus' garment, she was made whole from that hour.

> *And, behold, a woman, which was diseased with an issue of blood twelve years, came behind him, and touched the hem of his garment:*
>
> *For she said within herself, If I may but touch his garment, I shall be whole.*
>
> *But Jesus turned him about, and when he saw her, he said, Daughter, be of good comfort; thy faith hath made thee whole. And the woman was made whole FROM THAT HOUR.*
>
> (Matthew 9:20-22)

This healing involved the woman's faith; this is called faith healing.

Sometimes when people are prayed for, they do not see the results right away. But we must recognize that we are healed before we see the healing. This is real faith. We thank the Father for the healing *before* we see it. Remember, *"Now faith is the substance of things hoped for, the evidence of things not seen"* (Hebrews 11:1). Sometimes, the gifts of healing take time. The working of miracles are manifested immediately.

Thank God Ahead of Time

About six months after leaving the hospital, I caused the bone in my right ankle to slip out of place. I had jumped from a porch, and I knew at once that I was in trouble. I immediately began to pray and thank the Lord for my healing of this ankle ahead of time.

I had read about Jesus thanking the Father before the five loaves and two fish were turned into enough to feed a multitude.

> *And Jesus took the loaves; and when he HAD GIVEN THANKS, he distributed to the disciples, and the disciples to them that were set down; and likewise of the fishes as much as they would.* (John 6:11)

And, when Lazarus was raised from the dead, Jesus thanked the Father ahead of time:

> *Then they took away the stone from the place where the dead was laid. And Jesus lifted up his eyes, and said, FATHER, I THANK THEE that thou hast heard me.*
> *And when he thus had spoken, he cried with a loud voice, Lazarus, come forth.*
> (John 11:41, 43)

I was taken to an orthopedic surgeon. An x-ray was taken of my ankle. It was decided that surgery was needed, and this was set for one week later.

The next day I found a Holy Spirit revival in progress at church. I went up to the altar and asked the minister and the elders to pray that God would heal my ankle. After the prayer, I noticed that my foot was still swollen and still hurt. I asked the evangelist why this was so. He just told me to thank God ahead of time, and by faith God would do the impossible.

For three days I walked around limping and thanking God for my healing. People laughed at me because I was believing for my ankle to be healed. On the fourth morning, I got out of bed, and when my feet hit the floor, I knew I was healed! I started shouting and praising the Lord, because faith had now become reality!

About two hours later, the orthopedic surgeon called me on the telephone. He asked me if I remembered seeing the bone out of place on the x-ray he had taken.

I said, "Yes, doctor, but I got in a healing line, and Jesus healed my ankle; no surgery is needed now."

He asked me to repeat what I had said. I did. After a moment of silence, he told me he had just looked at my x-ray again, and it now showed the bone no longer out of place.

I said, "See there, doctor, not only can Jesus heal my body, but He can also heal your x-ray!" He said he had never seen such a thing in all his career, that this was truly a miracle. I told him that I give God the credit for all these works.

7

The Day I Met an Angel

After I began driving my car again, I picked up an old man on the side of the road that was hitchhiking. I now believe this man was an angel. Let me explain.

When he got into the car, we began to talk about Jesus. He told me he was traveling ninety miles north. I felt the need to help him, so I told him I would drive him there. In Matthew 25:40, Jesus said, *"Inasmuch as ye have done it unto one of the least of these my brethren, ye have done it unto me."* I was clueless on what was about to happen.

When we got to where he wanted to go, he grabbed his suitcase as he got out of the car. Then he did a very strange thing. He put his hand to his head, as if something was wrong. He trotted back over to the car. He told me he had left his walking cane on the side of the road where I had picked him up. I told him to forget that one, and I reached into the back of my car to give him mine. It was a gold-colored duck head cane my mother had given to me as a present. I told him to keep it and use it. He took it and thanked me. I told him I would get another one.

Then the man did another strange thing. He sat down on his suitcase in the middle of the yard. As I was backing out of the driveway, I stopped and asked him why he did not go on into the house. He said he could not go in at that time. He smiled and waved good-bye, and I did the same.

I thought about this all the way home. When I got almost home, I heard the Lord say Hebrews 13:2. I opened my Bible and read it aloud. The thought then came to me that he might have been an angel. The writer of Hebrews tells us,

> *"Be not forgetful to entertain strangers: for thereby some have entertained angels unawares"*
> (Hebrews 13:2).

I pulled into the driveway at home, and I got out running and shouting, telling the story of this old man. About a half-hour later, my aunt asked me where my walking stick was, and why was I not limping. All of a sudden, I looked down and realized I had been walking without my cane. I started worshipping God for delivering me from the cane. God healed me as I had compassion on someone else. The Lord will set us up sometimes just to bless us. I have not needed support in my walking since that day—since the day I met an angel.

A Tumor Disappears Overnight

*J*esus told me one day why He heals people in various ways. He said, "Son, I know how I can receive the most glory for My works, and I will share My glory with no man."

I believe that many people notice or receive their miracle of healing when they are by themselves, so that only Jesus will get the credit. I prayed for a woman in a revival meeting in West Memphis, Arkansas. She had a tumor on her side the size of a small melon. I told her that she was healed. She said, "How can you say that when this thing is still here on my side?"

I explained how God heals us by faith, and how to accept the healing ahead of time. She said she felt like she would be lying if she told someone she was healed, when the tumor was still present. I told her to thank the Lord anyway.

The next night she came to church shouting that it had worked. The tumor had disappeared overnight! What touched my heart was her husband. He was behind her, crying. He said, "Brother Madison, I've been away from God for thirteen years, but I've seen a miracle here in my wife, and I'm coming back home to Jesus!"

This is why Jesus is still in the miracle-working business. Mark 11:24 tells us, *"Therefore I say unto you, What things soever ye desire, when ye pray, believe that ye receive them, and ye shall have them."* Whether it takes a minute, an hour, a week, or a month, consider it done when you pray, and thank Him ahead of time. This is how I revealed to this lady how to receive. We are told in Hebrews 11:6,

> **But without faith it is impossible to please him: for he that cometh to God must believe that he is, and that he is a rewarder of them that diligently seek him.**

I believe that He is, indeed, a rewarder of those who seek Him diligently. I believe this, and I diligently seek Him. It is through Him that I am able to do everything that I do. He gives us the power to overcome. So why not come to Jesus today? Be healed spiritually, physically, and emotionally. He awaits you!

Dreams and Visions

And it shall come to pass in the last days, saith God, I will pour out of my Spirit upon all flesh: and your sons and daughters shall prophesy, and your young men shall see visions, and your old men shall dream dreams.
(Acts 2:17)

After running out of my wheelchair, I really started reading the Bible with more intensity. I could not get enough of what God has said and what He is saying. I believe the days that we live in now are the last days. I believe that God is pouring out His Spirit upon all people. I believe that these final days will usher in the greatest harvest of souls that this world has ever seen.

This is the latter rain that Jesus has been waiting for. Jesus has great patience, and He is coming again to receive the early rain and latter rain.

Be patient therefore, brethren, unto the coming of the Lord. Behold, the

*husbandman waiteth for the precious fruit
of the earth, and hath long patience for it,
until he receive the early and latter rain.*
(James 5:7)

The rain represents people of all nations, tongues, and creeds. Before Jesus comes for His bride, that is, for anyone who believes in His shed blood, He must pour out His Spirit. This is why we have seen Communism begin to fall and walls begin to crumble and religious freedom ignited in the Third World countries. Only recently, millions of people have come to know Jesus for the first time.

Just as I have learned about healing by receiving healing, I have learned about dreams and visions by having dreams and visions. I could not make myself have dreams and visions, nor could I force God to give them to me. Oh, but I could make myself hungry for God!

Jesus tells us in Matthew 5:6, *"Blessed are they which do hunger and thirst after righteousness: for they shall be filled."* And, He says in verse eight, *"Blessed are the pure in heart: for they shall see God."*

I believe that some conditions have to be met in order for people to receive dreams and visions from God. First, they have to be born again. Secondly, they must do what is right and avoid evil. Thirdly, they need to read the Word of God and keep His commandments. Finally, they have to worship God in spirit and in truth.

I knew I would have dreams—regular dreams—but I never thought I would have the kind of dreams I have had. And I had no idea I would ever have visions. Many times a vision happens when a person is awake and aware of their surroundings. A picture or event begins to unfold before their eyes.

Some people ask me how they can hear the voice of God. First of all, God speaks to us by His Word. Here are two key verses from the Scriptures that help to crystallize this fact:

God, who at sundry times and in divers manners spake in time past unto the fathers by the prophets,
Hath in these last days spoken unto us by his Son, whom he hath appointed heir of all things, by whom also he made the worlds;
(Hebrews 1:1-2)

In the beginning was the Word, and the Word was with God, and the Word was God.
(John 1:1)

Secondly, God speaks to us through His servants and ministers. Paul wrote in his letters to the Ephesians and Corinthians:

And he gave some, apostles; and some, prophets; and some, evangelists; and some, pastors and teachers;
For the perfecting of the saints, for the work of the ministry, for the edifying of the body of Christ:
(Ephesians 4:11-12)

And God hath set some in the church, first apostles, secondarily prophets, thirdly teachers, after that miracles, then gifts of healings, helps, governments, diversities of tongues.
(1 Corinthians 12:28)

Hear now my words: If there be a prophet among you, I the Lord will make

myself known unto him in a vision, and will
speak to him in a dream.

(Numbers 12:6)

God also reveals Himself and His will by His Spirit:

How that by revelation he made known
unto me the mystery; (as I wrote afore in few
words,
Whereby, when ye read, ye may
understand my knowledge in the mystery of
Christ)
Which in other ages was not made
known unto the sons of men, as it is now
revealed unto his holy apostles and prophets
by the Spirit;

(Ephesians 3:3-5)

But when the Comforter is come, whom
I will send unto you from the Father, even
the Spirit of truth, which proceedeth from the
Father, he shall testify of me:

(John 15:26)

Howbeit when he, the Spirit of truth, is
come, he will guide you into all truth: for he
shall not speak of himself; but whatsoever
he shall hear, that shall he speak: and he will
shew you things to come.

(John 16:13)

No matter how God chooses to reveal Himself to us, we will still hear Him if we are following Him closely. Jesus said, *"My sheep hear my voice"* (John 10:27).

My First Dream of Instruction

In the first dream I had from the Lord, I saw myself lifted up from the floor, and my uncle came into the room where my dad and I were. My uncle was speaking in another language. My dad said, "Son, come down from there."

I said, "Dad, this is the power of God holding me up; the Lord is trying to show you His power. Look at Uncle Joe and listen. He is speaking in another language, just as they did on the Day of Pentecost." Then I woke up.

The book of Acts reveals the events of the Day of Pentecost:

> *And when the day of Pentecost was fully come, they were all with one accord in one place.*
> *And suddenly there came a sound from heaven as of a rushing mighty wind, and it filled all the house where they were sitting.*
> *And there appeared unto them cloven tongues like as of fire, and it sat upon each of them.*
> *And they were all filled with the Holy Ghost, and began to speak with other tongues, as the Spirit gave them utterance.*
> (Acts 2:1-4)

What a great power filled these believers! In Acts 19:6, we read, "And when Paul had laid his hands upon them, the Holy Ghost came on them; and they spake with tongues, and prophesied." This was truly a sign that Christ had not left them comfortless, but He had given the Spirit who had been promised.

> *Wherefore tongues are for a sign, not to them that believe, but to them that believe not: but prophesying serveth not for them that believe not, but for them which believe.*
> (1 Corinthians 14:22)

About a week later, as I was in prayer, the Lord spoke to me about this dream. The Lord said, "Son, the dream you had was not for your dad, or to let you know that your uncle will receive the baptism of My Spirit. Rather, it was to let you know that it does not matter what I enable you to do; there will still be people who do not believe."

I had been praying for God to enable me to do something out of the ordinary to help some of my family members believe in the Lord. But if they did not believe that God is real after seeing me in the hospital's ICU and looking at me now, then they might never believe.

Many people do believe in God, and they know Jesus is real, but they do not serve Him by keeping His commandments and going to church. I now understand that I cannot convince everyone to believe, even though that is my desire. I learned a similarly valuable lesson in each of my dreams and visions.

My Second Dream of Instruction

The second dream the Lord gave me was for the purpose of teaching me about the name of Jesus. I dreamed that I was out in an open pasture and that a young man was standing next to me. I said to him, "Watch this, brother. In the name of Jesus, let the sun come down, and the rain also."

It started to rain, and the sun went behind a mountain. The young man covered his head and asked me if I could make it stop raining. I told him I could not, but the name of Jesus could. I raised my hand and said, "In the name of Jesus, let the rain stop, and let the sun come back up."

I looked over at the young man and said to him, "This is a miracle, but you do not have to operate in the gift of miracles to see miracles happen. Just use the name of Jesus. The power is in the name!"

Then I woke up and realized I had been dreaming. Suddenly, God spoke to my heart. He said, "Do you understand what I have shown you?"

I answered, "Yes, Lord, I do. I can stop asking You to help me operate in the gift of miracles, and I can start speaking Your name and see the miracles."

Jesus said, "The gifts of the Spirit are still in operation today because My Spirit is here on earth to bring them about. If you will seek to prophesy, to comfort and edify My people, and to let love be foremost in your life and ministry, I will use you in great ways."

I believe the young man in the dream was also a type of church, because when the rain began to fall, he covered himself up. Many churches in this day and time need an outpouring of the spiritual rain, but when God sends a move of the Holy Spirit their way, they cover up and refuse to get involved. Therefore, they are left dry.

Walking on Water

One night, while I was praying at my bedside, God impressed me to go down to the small lake behind the house and walk across the water. At first, I laughed and said, "Surely You're not serious. Lord, only You and Peter walked on the water. I need to wake everyone up to see this because they will not believe it." I let doubt arise. I continued to pray, and I tried to make a deal with God. If it was really He who told me to walk on the water, then I wanted Him to have someone come up to me the next day and tell me he or she believed that God was still able to cause people to walk on the water.

The very next day, I was in Jasper, Alabama, about eighteen miles north of my home. I saw a woman there whom I knew from a church I visited often, and she said, "Hello, Brother Rick, I dreamed of that catfish lake behind your home last night. I saw you walk past the pier and out onto the water."

"You dreamed this last night?" I inquired.

"Yes, I did," she replied.

I got so excited about what she had said that I drove all the way back home praising the Lord. I forgot to buy the supplies I had gone after and had to go back to town. I was delighted to know that I had found favor in the sight of God.

I did not walk on the water, but I know I could, if I had to. Faith in the name of Jesus will allow us to do all things. Many people have asked me how they can be used by God more and hear His voice more. I believe we must walk in the Spirit continuously if we want to be used by God continuously. Walking in the Spirit allows us to see the miraculous!

The Power of God

To do this, we need the baptism of the Holy Spirit, as recorded in the book of Acts. Jesus never did any miracles until He had received the Holy Spirit. John the Baptist saw the Spirit descend from heaven in the form of a dove and rest upon Jesus. *"And John bare record, saying, I saw the Spirit descending from heaven like a dove, and it abode upon him"* (John 1:32).

Some Christians today say that the baptism of the Holy Spirit and speaking in other tongues are not for us, because we have the Word today. But Jesus is the Word. The very first verse of John's gospel is about Jesus being the living Word of God: *"In the beginning was the Word, and the Word was with God, and the Word was God."* First John 5:7 says, *"For there are three that bear record in heaven, the Father, the Word, and the Holy Ghost: and these three are one."* Revelation 19:13 also tells us that Christ is the Word: *"And he was clothed with a vesture dipped in blood: and his name is called The Word of God."*

Jesus needed the fullness of the Holy Spirit before He turned the water into wine. This was His first miracle, as we are told in John 2:11:

> **This beginning of miracles did Jesus in Cana of Galilee, and manifested forth his glory; and his disciples believed on him.**

The apostle Paul put it best in 2 Corinthians 3:6, saying, *"*[God] *also hath made us able ministers of the new testament; not of the letter, but of the spirit: for the letter killeth, but the spirit giveth life."* God does things *"not by might, nor by power, but by* [His] *spirit"* (Zechariah 4:6). The Spirit of God will always agree with the Word. Everything He does will line up with and reveal the Word.

When we are born again, we receive the Spirit of God, as stated in Ephesians 1:13:

> **In [Christ] ye also trusted, after that ye heard the word of truth, the gospel of your salvation: in whom also after that ye believed, ye were sealed with that holy Spirit of promise.**

But sometimes we still may not receive the fullness of the Holy Spirit that is talked about in Acts 2:1-4 and in Ephesians 3:19. Why is this so? Because so many times we try to work our way into the power of the Spirit.

We are saved by grace, not by works. *"For by grace are ye saved through faith; and that not of yourselves: it is the gift of God"* (Ephesians 2:8). We cannot work our way into heaven or into His fullness, although keeping His commandments, which is something we do after we are saved, is sometimes called *works.* Of course, we do ask God to reveal to us His purpose and will for our lives. In Matthew 7:7, we are told, *"Ask, and it shall be given you; seek and ye shall find; knock, and it shall be opened unto you."*

Jesus commanded His disciples to wait in Jerusalem to be filled with the Holy Spirit: *"Behold, I send the promise of my Father upon you: but tarry ye in the city of Jerusalem, until ye be endued with power from on high"* (Luke 24:49). In Acts 1:8, Jesus said, *"But ye shall receive power, after that the Holy Ghost is come upon you."* The baptism of the Holy Spirit surely is for us in these times.

God Stops a Lady from Committing Suicide

In the third dream that God gave me, I saw a lady weeping, but I did not know her. I spoke to her in order to comfort her. I saw her face clearly.

The next day, the Holy Spirit led me to a restaurant in Birmingham, about forty-five miles east of my home. *"For as many as are led by the Spirit of God, they are the sons of God"* (Romans 8:14). As I walked into the restaurant, I saw the same woman who had been in my dreams the night before. I introduced myself. I told her that Jesus loved her and wanted to give her peace from the tragedies that she had faced recently.

I had never seen this lady before in my life. She told me her story. She told me about the death of her father; she told me about her husband leaving her; she told me that she was going to commit suicide. But she wound up giving her heart to Jesus instead.

I know our steps are ordered by the Lord: *"The steps of a good man are ordered by the Lord: and he delighteth in his way"* (Psalm 37:23). Ananias was sent to Saul, who later became Paul. Ananias had a vision from God, which we can read about in Acts 9:10:

And there was a certain disciple at Damascus, named Ananias; and to him said the Lord in a vision, Ananias. And he said, Behold, I am here, Lord.

Paul later wrote two-thirds of the New Testament under the leadership of the Holy Spirit. He said he would *"come to visions and revelations"* (2 Corinthians 12:1), but he said he would not be exalted by them, because it was God who gave them.

Sometimes we eat too much before we go to sleep, and our stomachs and intestines have to work overtime in order to digest the food. This causes us to have dreams, sometimes even nightmares. Not every dream is from heaven. But if it is from the Lord, you will know it. And if it has a message in it for you or for someone else, the Lord will reveal it.

God has given me the interpretation of other people's dreams and visions, but such ability comes with much prayer and fasting and a knowledge of the Word of God. *"When he, the Spirit of truth, is come, he will guide you into all truth...and he will shew you things to come"* (John 16:13).

My First Vision

In the first vision I had, I looked up toward the ceiling, and a white cloud began to unfold. It was about eleven o'clock at night in August of 1986; I had been reading the word of God all day and night for several days. It was like a movie projector started running on the ceiling.

Jesus appeared in the middle of the cloud with a white robe on. I could not see his face, but I just knew it was Jesus. He began to reveal to me about future world events. One event would be many Jewish people returning to Israel. Now, we know that over five hundred thousand returned to Israel from 1989 to 1991. The Lord also revealed that 1993 would be a very important year for Israel. I was amazed, as I watched on TV in 1993, Israel and her Arab neighbor signing a seven year peace treaty.

The Lord said Israel would sign two different seven year peace treaties. He compared these two agreements to Jacob, who made two seven year agreements with his Arab father-in-law. He did this in order to receive his wives Leah and Rachel:

> *"I will serve thee seven years for Rachel thy younger daughter."*
> (Genesis 29:18b)

> *Fulfil her week, and we will give thee this also for the service which thou shalt serve with me yet seven other years.*
> *And Jacob did so, and fulfilled her week: and he gave him Rachel his daughter to wife also.*
> (Genesis 29:27-28)

A week in Bible prophecy is seven years. The world is pressuring Israel to sign another peace treaty. It may take the war of Ezekiel 38 and 39 to bring about the final seven year treaty spoken in Daniel 9:27. I believe God is warning people to get ready for his soon return. We shall meet him in the air.

For the Lord himself shall descend from heaven with a shout, with the voice of the archangel, and with the trump of God: and the dead in Christ shall rise first:

Then we which are alive and remain shall be caught up together with them in the clouds, to meet the Lord in the air: and so shall we ever be with the Lord.

(1 Thessalonians 4:16-17)

Behold, I shew you a mystery; We shall not all sleep, but we shall all be changed,

In a moment, in the twinkling of an eye, at the last trump: for the trumpet shall sound, and the dead shall be raised incorruptible, and we shall be changed.

(1 Corinthians 15:51-52)

Jesus told me to go all over the world and tell everyone, that He is coming soon. One of the reasons the Lord raised me up from my deathbed, was to warn people to repent, and seek the living God.

Another world event Jesus revealed to me was on Sept. 10, 2001. I was preaching in a church in Dyer, Tennessee. I was conducting a revival and the Lord was doing marvelous things. I heard the following words in my spirit, "Tomorrow the world will change and many will watch it on the news. People from the Middle East will be involved." We all remember what happened on September 11, 2001.

This date is now referred to as nine-eleven. The next night, the church had standing room only, and many wanted to know what I had said. Amos tells us that God warns his people first, *"Surely the Lord God will do nothing, but he revealeth his secret unto his servants the prophets"* (Amos 3:7).

Future Terrorist Acts

I have also been shown by the Spirit of God that explosions will happen across America from coast to coast by terrorists. Jesus told me that he had allowed Hurricane Katrina in New Orleans to bring a cleansing to the city, and to help our government learn how to prepare for future city wide disasters. I revealed this to several people in a meeting in Tennessee.

While I was explaining about future disasters, the Lord said to tell everyone there would be an earthquake in Tennessee very soon. I received a phone call the very next day that an earthquake had occurred in Athens, Tennessee. I believe Jesus was showing everyone that I was speaking the truth. We need to fast and pray for our family and friends.

On the day of Pentecost, Peter stood and quoted what the prophet Joel had spoken, "But Peter, standing up with the eleven, lifted up his voice and said unto them, AND IT SHALL COME TO PASS IN THE LAST DAYS, SAITH GOD, I WILL POUR OUT OF MY SPIRIT UPON ALL FLESH: AND YOUR SONS AND YOUR DAUGHTERS SHALL PROPHESY, AND YOUR YOUNG MEN SHALL SEE VISIONS, AND YOUR OLD MEN SHALL DREAM DREAMS."

(Acts 2:14a, 17)

Dreams and visions still occur, because God is still pouring out His Spirit upon all flesh. If we will seek the Lord, read His word, and pray, we will hear from heaven. Fasting and praying puts us in a place to receive from the Lord. It helps us to be spiritually minded.

My Second Vision

In the second vision I had, I looked toward the ceiling, and I began to see myself walking down long hallways and opening doors. I could feel the presence of the Lord so strongly. I was wide awake, and this vision was so clear. I said aloud, "Lord, where are you taking me?" Jesus replied, "This is not about where you are going, but rather what you are doing. I am opening doors for you, and you are going through them." The Lord told me to name my ministry Operation Healing Ministry. He told me to give all the glory for accomplishments to Him. I do!

My Third Vision

I had my third vision after I walked out of the wheelchair. I saw an orange cloud begin to roll on the floor. Inside this cloud, a picture began to unfold. I saw myself in church. All of a sudden the pastor asked for a healing line. I walked up to the altar, and six other people were standing next to me. The vision faded away. I said, "Lord, what are You saying to me? Is there a particular church You want me to go to tomorrow?"

Jesus never said anything, but I got the message. The next morning, Sunday, I decided I would get ready and visit a church about ten blocks down the street. I had spent the night with some friends, and I had explained salvation to them. One friend had to go to work on this particular morning. The other was sick. I did not have my car at this time, so I had no way of getting to church. But God was my provider. I asked the Lord to send some transportation. After I got ready, I stood at the front door and said, "Okay, Lord, I'm ready."

A man whom I had met before my accident pulled into the driveway. He got out and walked up to the door. I got in on the passenger side of his truck. He was still standing at the door of the house. I rolled the window down and said, "Come on, brother, you've got to take me down the street to church."

He said, "I'm fifteen minutes late to be somewhere now, and I have to go twenty more minutes down the interstate. I don't even know why I got off the interstate." I told him he had done the right thing. He came back to the truck, got in, and took me to church. I told him while we were driving that I would get a ride back to the house. I also told him about all the miracles that had happened in my life since the accident. He was amazed that I was still alive, much less walking. I thanked him and bid him good-bye and walked into the church.

When I walked into the church, the first thing I saw was orange carpet. I knew I had walked into the orange cloud. The pastor asked for a healing line before he preached. I had seen all this happend the night before. But I sat down and watched in amazement instead of getting involved.

I let the enemy talk me out of a blessing. The Devil said to me, "You don't have to get in that healing line. Besides, people will look at you with this cane and make fun of you." I felt as if Jesus was pressing me to go up to the altar for healing. But I found out that when people are visiting a church for the first time, they often have a tendency to hold back.

I learned from this experience never to be embarrassed or ashamed about my faith, even if I do not know anyone in the room. I was angry at myself. Later, I gave my testimony there, and several people were saved. Praise God! God can reveal to us that He wants us to be blessed, but we have to do our part. We must press in and receive.

The book of Joel describes an army that God will raise up in the last days—an army that will march through the land and conquer the enemy: *"A great people and a strong; there hath not been ever the like, neither shall be any more after it, even to the years of many generations"* (Joel 2:2). Even Daniel stated that great exploits will follow those who know their God: *"But the people that do know their God shall be strong, and do exploits"* (Daniel 11:32). Why not seek God with prayer and fasting, and see what He reveals to you?

Instruction from the Voice of God

One evening the Lord spoke to my heart, and he told me to get in my car and drive. I had heard of walking by faith, but this was driving by faith. After driving for about forty minutes, I heard the Lord say, "Turn down this road, and don't stop." I immediately turned and drove several miles."

I thought about Abraham, and how God told him to go into a land that he did not know. Abraham walked by faith and God rewarded him for his faith and patience.

I looked down and noticed that the gas gauge was nearly on empty. I said, "Jesus, I hope this was you that brought me out into the wilderness. This must be a test." I noticed an outside light and several cars just down the street. As I pulled up, I saw a church full of people. After parking and walking in, I noticed a gospel singing had already started. An usher took me to the only seat available, which happened to be on the front row. After sitting down, I heard the Lord tell me to pray for the man on my left. I looked at him and smiled, and tried to see what might be wrong with him. The Lord impressed me again to pray for the man.

All of a sudden, the Holy Spirit stood me up in front of the man. My thought was, "Why didn't I just reach over and pray for him, because now everyone was looking at me." I laid my hand on his head and began to pray. He leaped up and began to jump up and down. He then hugged me, and thanked me for obeying the Lord.

I asked the man what had been his problem, and he said he was recovering from back surgery. The surgery did not remove the pain. The Lord had instructed him to go to this church that night, and he would be healed. Immediately, he felt no pain, and could bend over and touch his toes. Neither of us had ever been to this church before. When I left I had one-fourth of a tank of gas! God is so good!

One day while driving through Alabama, the Holy Spirit suddenly instructed me to exit the interstate. I drove through a small town called Warrior, Alabama. I heard the Lord say, "Stop at that white house on the left and pray for the sick man." I had never been there before, nor did I know anyone who lived there.

After knocking on the door, an elderly lady appeared. I told her the Lord Jesus had instructed me to stop and pray for somebody. She immediately grabbed my arm, and hurried me into a back room, where her son was lying on the floor. He had been an alcoholic all his life. He was experiencing hallucinations, also known as going through DT's. I laid my hand on his head and began to pray.

He immediately stopped vomiting and shaking. He sat up and he was as sober as could be. He began to cry, and started asking me questions regarding who I was. I then led him in the prayer of salvation and he was instantly a new man. His mother said she had been praying to God for help. She wanted to know if I was an angel. I explained that I was just a man trying to obey the voice of God.

One day the Lord instructed me to go to a hospital in Birmingham, Alabama. Jesus said He wanted to use me to perform some miracles. Little did I know that He wanted me to raise people up out of comas. I walked into the elevator expecting to hear where I should depart. The 10th floor was where the doors opened and the action soon began.

I had no clue that the ICU department had temporarily moved to the top floor, due to construction. After exiting the elevator, I saw a sign that read ICU department. I went in, and a nurse met me. I told her I was there to pray for someone. She asked who I was there to see. I told her that Jesus had sent me, but He did not give me a name.

She looked at me like I was crazy, and sent me out in the hallway. The Lord said, "Go back in and don't be afraid." I went back in the ICU, but the nurse didn't see me, thank God. I began to pray and lay hands on the first patient I came to. I was watching and praying, by keeping one eye on the nurse, and the other closed in prayer. When I opened my eyes, the patient had his eyes open. I told him that Jesus was healing him, and to give Him all the glory.

Then I went to the next patient, and the same thing happened. A lady in the corner asked me to come pray for her son. She said, "My son is in a coma also. If God can wake those people up, then He can wake my child up." She explained that the other two people had been in comas and one had not opened their eyes in twenty-three days, and the other for twelve days. I reached down and touched her son's foot, and immediately he awoke out of the coma.

Then the nurse saw me and I moved swiftly toward the door. The Lord told me that Elijah did the same thing. He called fire down one moment, and ran from a woman the next (1 Kings 19).

I have prayed for many people in comas, and at least fourteen have awakened out of comas. I have seen several people walk out of wheelchairs. I know of numerous occasions where people have been healed and delivered of cancer. I have prayed for many people who have received their eye sight and hearing. To God be the Glory!

In one service, the Lord instructed me to put my finger in a lady's deaf ear and pray for her. After praying, I covered up her other ear, and begin to ask her to repeat after me. She could hear perfectly. She then told the church that she had no ear drum, but she could hear!

A Word About the Courts

In April of 2005, the Lord spoke to me early one morning. He said that He was about to bring changes to the court system in America. I told several friends what the Lord had said. Within a few months, new judges were getting elected in several states. These judges were considered conservative with moral and Christian backgrounds. Then, later in the year the Supreme Court was getting a new Chief Justice. Judge Roberts is considered by many to be a strong conservative. Then President Bush had to select two more candidates to join the Supreme Court in 2006. My friends reminded me that God had truly spoken a word about the court systems. Hopefully, God is sending revival to our state and federal governments.

Financial Miracles

> **But my God shall supply all your need according to his riches in glory by Christ Jesus.**
>
> (Philippians 4:19)

I have found the above passage to be a part of my life and ministry. Sometime after the accident, I walked to a small church across the street from my dad's house in Nashville, Tennessee. I was still walking with a cane at this time. I shared my testimony of how God had raised me from the dead. I felt led to give the pastor an offering. I only had $7, and I needed all I could scrape up just to get back to Alabama. The Lord impressed me to give $5, but I only wanted to give $2. However, I obeyed the Lord and gave the $5 to the pastor. The Lord said He would supply all my needs.

Right after that, I went to visit the people with whom I had lived before I was in the wreck. I had forgotten about putting $1,058 in a sock and hiding it in one of the dresser drawers I had used there, but the Lord had not forgotten. While I was testifying to my ex-roommates, the Lord told me to go and get a pair of socks. I wore sandals at this time, because socks and shoes hurt my ankle. I thought God was saying that the nerves in my feet and legs were going to be healed when I put the socks on.

I went to the dresser drawer, and I grabbed a pair of socks. I felt something rolled up in them. As I opened the socks, there was $1,058. About $788 was in the form of a check, and about $270 was in cash.

I had had my own air-conditioning business, and I had missed making a deposit on Friday, April 11, 1986. The head-on collision occurred on April 13, 1986, a Sunday morning.

In just two hours, God turned $5 into $270 in cash. The check was past ninety days old, so I sent it back to the company that had issued it. They sent me a new check within five days, and they also sent an additional check that they said they owed me. I told them that my records did not indicate this, but they insisted that I keep the payment. So, by obeying the Lord in a five dollar offering, I received $1,300 back from God.

I repaired my car and used the rest to travel and preach the Gospel of Jesus Christ. If we give bountifully, we will receive bountifully (2 Corinthians 9:6). God said we are to bring our tithes into the storehouse, so that there may be meat. He said, *"Prove me now herewith...if I will not open you the windows of heaven, and pour you out a blessing, that there shall not be room enough to receive it"* (Malachi 3:10). It is God's will for us to be in health and to prosper (3 John 1:2).

I had a hospital bill of more than $180,000, and Jesus told me that if I would testify of His grace and healing power, He would take care of the hospital bill. I had no insurance, but when I started testifying of Jesus, the hospital bill was paid. It pays to be obedient to the Lord. *"Behold, to obey is better than sacrifice, and to hearken than the fat of rams"* (1 Samuel 15:22).

In May of 1989, I began conducting a revival in Panama City, Florida. I was traveling at the time in a fifteen foot travel trailer. God was about to fulfill a great need in my ministry. A dear sister in the Lord, Sister Davis, came to me one morning during the day service. We were having services morning and night. She said the Lord had prompted her to help me get a bigger travel trailer.

This was an answer to prayer. Amazingly, I had walked around a travel trailer in an RV sales center just two weeks earlier. I was doing a Jericho march around a travel trailer, when a salesman came up to me, and handed me a business card. I explained to him I was praying and believing for my God to provide according to His riches in glory. The salesman laughed and walked away. However, Jesus gave me exactly what I asked for.

The day Sister Davis told me her plan, I found a travel trailer—a 1987, thirty-one foot, Holiday Rambler Deluxe XLT. A Spirit-filled dentist was selling it for $17,000. Sister Davis told him I was an evangelist, and he knocked it down to $13,000. It was only three months old. Sister Davis gave him a check for $13,000, and told me to pay her back a little at a time. I paid her back $8,000 and one day she called me and said not to send anymore money. Hallelujah!

I felt that God wanted to do something for Sister Davis. She told me that her grandmother was in the nursing home, and she had never been saved. I went to visit her grandmother the next day. She asked Jesus to come into her heart, and it all seemed so easy. Sister Davis' grandmother passed away about one week later, but we know she is in heaven in the presence of the Lord!

God Makes a Way

Several years ago, I ran out of money while traveling. I didn't even have any change to buy a drink out of a machine. I started praying about what to do, and the Lord told me to open the trunk of my car. I saw a sack that I did not recognize. Upon opening it, I saw a lot of nickels, dimes, and quarters. I counted forty dollars. Suddenly, I had plenty of money to get home on, and buy something to drink. I had studied about the meaning of numbers in the Bible. I understood that the number forty means testing. I assumed the Lord was checking out my character once again. I have come to realize, that our reaction to any given situation reveals our maturity. It seems like the Lord allows situations to occur, then he makes a way of escape. He then rewards us for standing on faith.

He gives us the faith, and then blesses us for believing Him to do the impossible. Jesus wants His people to be blessed. Psalms 84:11 tells us, *"no good thing will he withhold from them that walk uprightly."*

In 1991, I began to pray and agree with many others that the Lord would bring a financial miracle. I believed for the Lord to move on someone's heart to bring my ministry out of debt, and help me buy some television equipment. I had already begun to build a 1,200 square foot television studio.

I started sowing seed by giving to other ministries. At the end of 1991, God spoke to a faithful Christian family to help my ministry. They gave $17,000 to Operation Healing Ministry. This brought the ministry out of debt, and gave me $7,000 to use on television equipment.

While preaching in Dalton, Georgia, that same week, I found $30,000 worth of TV equipment. Mr. Parker, who owned the equipment, said God wanted me to have it. He sold it to me for $7,000.00 that week. This included three three-quarter inch Panasonic cameras, two tripods, two slave masters for Super VHS editing, a mixing board, and lights. Remember, God will supply your needs.

In 1989 I needed to go to the dentist. I did not have a regular dentist at this time, so I made an appointment with a dentist near my home. While I was sitting in the lobby, God told me that this was not the dentist I should use. I cancelled my visit and drove up the highway several miles, where I spotted another dentist's office.

I went in and explained what I needed to have done. I also gave my testimony to several of the employees. While sitting in the dental chair, I asked Jesus to let this work not cost much because I had very little cash.

Jesus said, "Why don't you believe for it to be free? Believe for it, and I will perform it." I told the Lord that nobody goes to the dentist and gets free dental work, especially when it is your first visit and you do not know the dentist. But I said okay, and I thanked Jesus ahead of time for doing it. But in the back of my mind, I thought it was impossible.

When it came time to pay the bill, the statement said, "No charge." I asked the receptionist why, and she said that Dr. Brown just decided not to charge me. I also found out that he is a brother in the Lord.

One night, in church, I agreed in prayer with a woman for a financial miracle of $7,500. She said she was losing her car and home due to medical bills.

The next day, she found a grocery sack on her porch. She thought someone had brought her some groceries, but upon looking in the bag, she saw piles of money. She counted $10,000.

Afraid that someone had robbed a bank, she reported it to the police. The police could not find the origin of the money; however, they would not return it to her. She got a lawyer, and he won it back in court. However, the lawyer charged $2,500. But this left her with exactly $7,500.

Many times, I have found $5, $10, and even $20 in my coat pockets or on my countertop. Remember, God will provide for us.

My mother gave a copy of my testimony to a man who was very poor. After reading it, he cried and said he wished he had some money to help our ministry. He had been taking people to the hospital with what little gas money he had.

Two hours later, the man won $10 million. He gave a lot away to different people. He gave me a check for $100. He could have done more, but I was thankful for what he gave. *"Give, and it shall be given unto you"* (Luke 6:38).

In January 2004, I spoke at a house meeting. There were about 100 people present from several different churches. The reverse drive had gone out of my 1995 Mazda Mini Van. I asked the Lord if He was trying to show me something. He said for me to keep going forward, don't go backwards. The Lord must have a sense of humor.

After praying for everyone at the house meeting, Brother Wilkin, who owned the house, asked me what I needed them to pray about. I told everyone to pray I get $1,400.00 to fix my transmission, or perhaps I could get a better vehicle. All of a sudden Brother Wilkin said that this was no big problem to solve. He then reached over to his son and asked for some keys. He handed me the keys to a 1997 Toyota Four Runner. I thought for a moment I might pass out.

One year later, a man from Arkansas asked me to go to Florida to pray for his friend in a coma. On the way back home that night Brother Moreland gave me $1,500.00 to get my Mazda repaired.

Brother Moreland was so excited that his friend opened her eyes, and began to follow him around the room. I told him that the Lord would raise her up. I repaired the Mazda, and later gave it to a couple that had a nursing home ministry. I gave away an old Toyota pickup in 1991. A few weeks later someone gave me a nice Ford truck. You can't out give God!

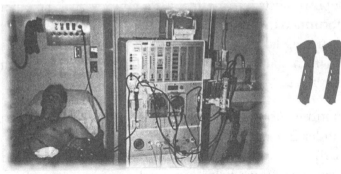

My Kidneys Fail

I had been preaching almost every day in 1991, and 1992 was booked solid four months in advance. My legs and feet had been swelling and holding a lot of fluid. I assumed I had been standing too much, so I cut down on my salt intake and propped my legs up during the day. Nothing seemed to help much. I had no idea that my kidneys were not working properly.

I began to lose my appetite, and nausea set in. In April 1992, my blood pressure went to 240 over 160, which is at stroke level. I had severe headaches, and I could not keep any food in my stomach. Finally, I went to the emergency room at a local hospital where I was diagnosed with renal (kidney) failure. I remained in the hospital for three days, but my condition got worse, so I was transported by ambulance to the hospital at the University of Alabama at Birmingham (UAB).

Many people were praying for me. I knew that Jesus would move on my behalf. I just did not know when or how. I remained in UAB for six days under one of the best renal nephrologists in America. After a biopsy was taken, it was determined that my kidneys had stopped working. The condition was labeled as chronic nephritis, or Bright's disease. I immediately had to go on dialysis so that my health could improve.

An intravenous access tube was inserted into the main artery under my collar bone. This allowed me to undergo dialysis three times a week—Monday, Wednesday, and Friday, for three and a half hours each session—once I got out of the hospital. I was still driving approximately two hundred miles per week for the ministry, even though the dialysis treatment consumed nearly three days each week.

I was again admitted into the hospital to be evaluated for a kidney transplant. UAB leads the world in kidney transplants, performing up to twenty per week. I was released after four days of testing, and I was approved for a transplant.

A person must be in good health to undergo a transplant. If I had a relative who could be a donor, then the transplant could be set up immediately. Several family members had decided to have their blood drawn to see if a match could be found. Donors are rated between one and six, with six being a perfect match. My mother was a match of four. My dad was later ruled out because he had only one lung. My mother went into the hosptial to be evaluated to make sure she was healthy enough to be a donor. She was approved.

I continued to preach in order to fulfill my obligations. I also continued with the dialysis in order to feel better. I could barely get my shoes on before dialysis, but after dialysis started, twenty pounds of fluid were removed.

I continued seeing miracles and healings in my revivals, but could not understand why God was not healing me. I thought of what the apostle Paul told the Corinthians, *"We are weak, but ye are strong"* (1 Corinthians 4:10). I felt weak, but Jesus was showing Himself strong in my weakness. I remembered Paul had asked the Lord to deliver him from a thorn in the flesh (2 Corinthians 12). The Lord had turned him down three times saying that His grace was sufficient (verses 7-9). I felt the Lord telling me the same thing.

Truly His grace is sufficient, but most of us want God to do things our way. In Psalm 34:19, the psalmist said, *"Many are the afflictions of the righteous: but the Lord delivereth him out of them all."* I comforted myself at times by reading how Paul went through many trials, beatings, persecutions, and even hunger for the Gospel. Why should I have thought I would escape any trials? All who live godly lives will suffer persecutions (2 Timothy 3:12), but God's grace is sufficient for every trial.

Soul Searching

I began to search within myself to see if I had done something wrong. I was sure I had, because I knew I was not perfect. I repented of my sins again. I even repented of things I had not done, just to make sure I would not prevent God from healing me. I asked for forgiveness for past, present, and future sins, although I knew I did not need to ask for forgiveness for my past sins.

The Lord said He would never remember our past once we repent. *"As far as the east is from the west, so far hath he removed our transgressions from us"* (Psalm 103:12). We might remember the past, but God puts our past into a sea of forgetfulness, never to be remembered again. *"And their sins and iniquities will I remember no more"* (Hebrews 10:17), says our God.

I evaluated my life. I did find cracks in my armor, where Satan could slip through and bombard my thoughts and actions. I prayed, and I sealed the cracks by reversing my statements or words. I knew I had made an opening for Satan with my words. Like the porter of the sheepfold in John 10, we can open the door to Jesus. Or, we can allow Satan to climb through an opening like a thief (verse 1).

> *But he that entereth in by the door is the shepherd of the sheep.*
> *To him the porter openeth; and the sheep hear his voice: and he calleth his own sheep by name, and leadeth them out.*
> (John 10:2-3)

Satan will force himself into the doors of our lives, but Jesus will never force Himself on us.

I realized that my life was in God's hands and that He was not going to let anything happen to me. Jesus had told me in January 1992 that He would use me to preach on television to millions of people. I knew that I could not die because the Lord was not finished with me yet. My situation was similar to Abraham's in Genesis 22, when God told him to kill Isaac, his only son. Abraham had been promised that he would be the father of many nations. Therefore, Abraham knew that God would raise Isaac from the dead if He had to, because God cannot lie. I could only believe and wait on God. I would not give up.

I trusted God with my life and my family. Even if God did not heal me, He is still the Healer and Deliverer. If I never saw another soul saved, He is still the Savior. He told me He was with me, and that was the only answer I needed. Good things come from above, for *"every good gift and every perfect gift...cometh down from the Father"* (James 1:17). God's ear is open to the righteous. His arm is not too short to reach down and touch us with compassion. *"Behold, the Lord's hand is not shortened, that*

it cannot save; neither his ear heavy, that it cannot hear"
(Isaiah 59:1).

I realized I had lost some of my zeal. I had grown calloused due to all the divisions in the body of Christ. I had built a wall around myself to protect myself from all the carnality and schisms. But it cost me my compassion. I prayed and fasted, but I could not seem to get back to my first love (Revelation 2:4). I also had not taken the best care of myself, pushing myself to three hundred days of preaching in 1991, and not eating properly. My condition seemed to be a combination of the accident in 1986, strep throat, which breaks down the kidneys, and, of course, Satan.

If we are in God's service, however, nothing can destroy us until God is through with us. I knew that God had a purpose for me and a calling on my life. *"And we know that all things work together for good to them that love God, to them who are the called according to his purpose"* (Romans 8:28). When Satan attacks us, we can know that God is about to use us.

A Decision Had to be Made

Many family members and friends wanted to be tested to be possible donors. Immediate family members are usually the only living donors that are used. However, spouses and friends had been approved as possible donors just prior to the time of my need. I kept putting the transplant off, believing that God would restore my own kidneys.

My mother felt led by God to be removed from the donor list. She had already been tested and approved, so it was a hard decision for her. I knew that she was strong in her faith and that she would do whatever Jesus said to do. We had no idea at the time that God wanted to use someone else as the donor.

I was anxious to get off of dialysis and be well again. I just knew that Jesus was not going to allow me to remain hooked up to a machine. I had work to do; I had to tell people all over the world that Jesus was real. I knew I could not do this and remain on dialysis. My thoughts for the moment went back to lying on a bed at UAB and watching so many people on dialysis. I knew the difference in my situation was that I was speaking the Word. There is power in our words! I knew deliverance belonged to me, and I tried to encourage everyone around me to do the same. Speak the Word!

A decision had to be made. My doctor gave me an ultimatum. I could either have a transplant, or have a graft surgically implanted in my forearm for dialysis. This graft is known as hemodialysis. I was not able to have peritoneal dialysis because my spleen had been removed.

We prayed for God's guidance. I had been against surgeries and operations to some degree, because so many people trust doctors more than they trust God. However, God wanted to bring some people at the hospital to salvation. He also wanted the seed of the Word planted in some particular doctors, nurses, and patients. He desired to use me to do the plowing, planting, and watering. (See 1 Corinthians 3:6.)

What a privilege to be used by God in any situation, even if it involves suffering. *"If we suffer, we shall also reign with him"* (2 Timothy 2:12). *"If so be that we suffer with him...we may be also glorified together"* (Romans 8:17). Do not misinterpret me. I do not like to suffer, and I certainly have had my share of suffering, but I know that trouble will come our way at times to try our faith. In each situation, God is faithful to provide a way out, so that we will be able to bear it.

There are times when it seems that we are going under. The devil will come in like a flood, but God will raise up a standard. He will always deliver us out of all of our difficult situations, even though it may seem impossible. As the Word tells us so.

> *There hath no temptation taken you but such as is common to man: but God is faithful, who will not suffer you to be tempted above that ye are able; but will with the temptation also make a way to escape, that ye may be able to bear it.*
> (1 Corinthians 10:13)

God was going to turn this situation around. Many people wonder why bad things happen to good people. God allows some things to happen to correct us and mature us. God's ways and thoughts are much higher than ours. *"For as the heavens are higher than the earth, so are my ways higher than your ways, and my thoughts than your thoughts"* (Isaiah 55:9). The end result is not often seen at the beginning. I never would have thought that God would take a drug addict and alcoholic like myself, raise me up from an automobile accident, and use me to save the lost and edify the church.

Africa Trip Cancelled

I was admitted to UAB hospital on July 16, 1992, to be prepped for surgery the next morning. I cancelled my missionary trip to Mexico and Nigeria. I was scheduled as the main speaker at a Holy Spirit rally in Nigeria. More than ten thousand people were expected. I could only pray that maybe next year I could fulfill this awesome task.

I was discouraged because I felt that I was disappointing a great many people. Then Jesus said to me, "I will finish what I have begun with you." These words were a confirmation of Philippians 1:6: *"He which hath begun a good work in you will perform it until the day of Jesus Christ."* I knew at this time that I would go through with the surgery. I felt the peace of God. No matter what happened, I was blessed, and I would be in the middle of more miracles. I would lift up the name of Jesus, even as Job lifted up the name of the Lord in the midst of his trials. *"Blessed be the name of the Lord"* (Job 1:21).

I had taken care of all my bills and responsibilities, and rescheduled all my revivals. I needed the help of many people, and everyone came through for me. Family and friends were so helpful and encouraging.

Delivered from the Machine

I had my final dialysis from eight o'clock in the morning until noon on July 16. If everything went well, I would never have to be on dialysis again. I knew in my heart that I was delivered from the machine, the artificial kidney. The machine cycles the blood through filters, and removes calories and energy from the patient.

I was amazed when I learned about the number of people who are on dialysis. Once they begin dialysis, many people are on it for the rest of their lives. We are so blessed in America with food that we are hurting the temple of God (our bodies) by eating too many fried foods and salts. We are not drinking enough water. Everyone should drink one or two quarts of water per day. I will never forget the day I was on dialysis, and a woman died next to me. She had been on dialysis for over twelve years, and it had taken a toll on her body. One day after I was removed from the dialysis machine, I passed out at the elevator. I came to, and the nurses were standing over me. I knew I had to tell them that I had just came from dialysis. I ended up staying at the hospital for five hours that day instead of three.

I felt very weak, but God had touched me every time I went on dialysis. While on this last dialysis, I thought about the three-day, four service revival I had just preached in Gadsden, Alabama. God had anointed me more than ever before. One alcoholic man had come down the aisle at the end of the Sunday night service to give his heart to the Lord. Three more people had re-dedicated their lives to Jesus. The revival would continue at the church, with Brother Dudley Smith singing and preaching for seven more days.

I wanted to meet Brother Smith and tell him how much I enjoyed watching him sing with John Starnes on television. A few days after the surgery, Brother Smith came to my hospital room with the pastor of the church that was hosting the revival. They had come to visit and to pray with me. Praise God, when we delight in Him, He will give us the desires of our hearts (Psalm 37:4).

A Miracle During Surgery

On Friday, July 17, 1992, at 7:00 A.M., I was rolled into a large cold operating room (OR). The plan was to make an incision on my right side near my appendix. The donor kidney would be placed near my pelvis, and attached upside down to my artery and bladder. This procedure worked best according to the doctors. The kidney sits in the pelvis, much like a baby in a cradle.

It was very cold in the OR, so warm blankets were placed over me. The anesthesiologist said that he would soon put me to sleep. I told him that God was with me and that I felt fine. I closed my eyes because of the brightness of the lamps, and God put me to sleep in a split second.

This must have been what Adam experienced when God put him to sleep (Genesis 2:21). When God put Adam to sleep and performed surgery on him, Adam felt no pain. I knew that even if something went wrong, I would not feel any pain. I don't think I ever went to sleep so fast and easy. Jesus is the best sleep doctor!

I awoke in the ICU department about six hours later, and family members took turns visiting me. They explained to me that the kidney began to work immediately. There were no complications. Three liters of urine had already been excreted, and my blood was being cleansed perfectly.

I am so grateful that the Lord delivered me from dialysis. All things work for good to them that love the Lord! I often think of the young man I led to Jesus in the hospital. I have a greater understanding now why the Apostle Paul said he took pleasure in infirmities, persecutions, and distresses for Christ's sake. When we are weak, then we are strong (2 Corinthians 12:10).

The anesthesiologist came to my room the next day. He told me that the operation was textbook material, and he rated it A-plus. He said the only problem during surgery was when my blood pressure dropped. He had to cut back on the anesthesia, and he had been afraid that I had felt the operation. He asked, "Did you feel any pain?"

I replied, "I never felt anything."

He said, "That is a miracle. Did you realize you went to sleep before I put you to sleep?"

"Yes, that was the peace of God," I answered.

Preaching in the ICU

I was awakened again at 4:00 P.M. on the day of my surgery by family and friends. It had been nine hours since the transplant. I felt great. I was giving all the glory to God. I felt like I could conquer the whole wide world again.

After visiting time was over, I could not fall back asleep, but I felt no pain. Although morphine had been prescribed for me every four hours, I stopped the nurses when it was time for the next dose I went ten hours without drugs. I was so full of the Holy Spirit that I could not shut up. For ten straight hours, I preached to the nurses and doctors. They heard my testimony about the auto accident in 1986. They saw the scars as proof. I explained about all the broken bones, infections and surgeries I experienced from the car wreck. They were all touched and amazed. The nurses said they were not used to patients waking up and talking to them the entire shift. I felt angels of God all around me.

I Leave the ICU Early

I was doing so well that I was transported to a private room the morning after the surgery. My own kidneys were left in my body. Now I had three kidneys. I was advised that the body could cleanse the blood with one kidney working. The Holy Spirit was working mightily through this third kidney. My IV was removed, and I was placed on anti-rejection drugs.

Eight out of ten transplant patients experience some kind of rejection. Our bodies know that something is in us that should not be there. I believed I would not experience any rejection because Jesus was my healer.

My body received a donor's kidney as its own. My creatinine level was 1.6, and my blood urea nitrogen (BUN) count was 33. The creatinine test determines the level of toxins that are in the blood. A creatinine level of one to two is perfect; anything higher than this would mean that the kidneys are reabsorbing too many toxins after trying to filter them.

The perfect BUN count for a male is 25 to 36. BUN refers to how much urea, a nitrogeous compound that comes from protein decomposition, is in the blood. Because my blood count and my creatinine levels were fine, my surgeon decided to reduce the anti-rejection drugs. He continued to reduce them for the entire week.

I thought it was wonderful to be improving so fast that medication was reduced immediately after surgery. I was up and out of bed Saturday night, the day after surgery. I counted twenty-seven staples in my right side. I moved slowly, because I did not want to pull any staples loose.

Remember, I had scars from the four-hundred staples from the surgeries, due to the automobile accident in 1986. Therefore, I was not concerned with the report of having more scars from staples. I was more concerned, but not worried, about having to walk the day after my surgery. I told the doctors that there was no way they were going to get me up the next day, and start walking. I later found out, that exercise is very good in helping someone recuperate after surgery. I did not get up and walk the next day. I did walk the second day, and it was painful!

Dismissed Early from the Hospital

I had improved so quickly that I was dismissed from the hospital just eight days after the transplant. I believe that numbers represent things in the same way that names have meanings. The number eight represents a new beginning. I was glad to get out on the eighth day.

Years earlier, UAB had purchased a nine-story apartment building called the Townhouse. Doctors and transplant recipients were allowed to stay there, so this is where I went after the eighth day in the hospital. This was very good for me. I could recover and be close to the hospital, which was all of one block away. I was able to see the transplant team several times a week, and I did not have to drive anywhere. UAB truly impressed me with their patient care and facilities.

I was escorted to the fourth floor in the Townhouse. All the patients on this floor were kidney recipients. I had a five-room apartment with a kitchen, a telephone, and a television. I was one and a half blocks from the cafeteria, with other eateries all around me. This was good news, since I had regained my appetite. I gained five pounds the first week.

UAB Hospital

I walked to the new $125 million doctors' clinic every morning, Monday through Friday, to have my blood drawn. The round trip was at least four blocks. Saturday morning I went to the hospital clinic. I had all day Sunday off and free time after 10:00 A.M. the rest of the days. Many of the other transplant patients had remained in the hospital for three to four weeks. On top of that, some had been in the Townhouse for the same amount of time.

I had trouble going to sleep at night because I was so excited and happy. I sensed angels were all around me. I could feel their presence. The Lord brought to my remembrance a friend of mine, Pastor Gensemer, who had recently started a church three blocks away. I called him and asked him to pick me up for the midweek service.

He asked me to share a few Scriptures with the congregation. God's anointing came upon me so strongly that I preached for thirty minutes. Pastor Gensemer then preached for thirty minutes, and we spent time dwelling in the presence of the Lord. *"I was glad when they said unto me, Let us go into the house of the Lord"* (Psalm 122:1). It was the fourteenth day since the surgery, and I was back at my Father's business.

I had not really ever stopped doing my Father's business. I had witnessed to fifty people, one-on-one, during the first ten days I was in the hospital, and three of them gave their lives to Jesus. A woman in housekeeping was sanctified and decided she would begin to seek more of God. All of my family witnessed to so many people, planting and watering the seed (Word) of God. We must realize where we are and why we are there at all times. *"The steps of a good man are ordered by the Lord"* (Psalm 37:23).

Witnessing to Coworkers at UAB

I looked at the window of my room in the Townhouse. I suddenly remembered working on the air-conditioning units below years ago. I was an a/c mechanic at UAB from 1980-1983. I had no idea I would ever be living in the Townhouse. I had hit the time clock just across the street for thirty-six months. As I wrote earlier, after I left UAB I moved to Tennessee, and later had my own business. Now I wanted to see my coworkers again so that I could tell them my testimony.

I had already witnessed to a former coworker at UAB. Now I could call the maintenance department at the Townhouse and witness to the workers about my new miracle. One friend said, "Gosh, Rick, every time I see you, you have a new addition to your testimony." Others said that I had definitely changed, or that I was lucky. I told them I was not lucky, but blessed.

Severed Brain-stem Healed

I think often about how blessed I am to have been given so many chances to live and appreciate life. When we think we have it bad, all we have to do is look around. One day, I went to Children's Hospital in Birmingham, Alabama, to pray for a young girl. Her condition looked hopeless. She had been in a car wreck, and she was diagnosed with a severed brain stem. Her family had been advised to prepare for a funeral. They believed in Jesus, but were not sure if it was God's will for their daughter to be healed.

I assured them it was God's will for Andrea to be healed. I went into the NICU department and I laid my hand on her head. As I was praying, her left leg began to jump, as if she was trying to get out of bed. Her mom and dad were watching very intently. I told them this was a sign that she was being healed. I told her family she would be coming home, not to make funeral arrangements. Five days later, I received the news that Andrea had gone home. She had no sign of a severed brain stem. Praise the name of Jesus.

One day, my mother and I prayed for a woman which had full blown aids. The woman only weighed about 80 pounds. We anointed her with oil, and prayed the prayer of faith. She was completely healed. The doctors have verified it. WHAT A GOD WE SERVE!!!!

12

What I Have Learned

My kidney transplant operation taught me several lessons, especially the lesson that healings, miracles, and prosperity are not all that the Gospel of Jesus Christ conisists of. In the last days, the church seems to be shouting *"peace and safety"* (1 Thessalonians 5:3), which, in our times, translates into compromise and materialism. It is indeed God's will for His church to be in health and to prosper, but only in His Way.

I have learned that God allows things to happen in our Christian walk in order to challenge our faith. It is obvious that God will use various ways to make us healthy—not because He has to, but because He chooses to. He knows what it will take to make us pure gold.

> *"For he is like a refiner's fire, and like fullers' soap; and he shall sit as a refiner and purifier of silver; and he shall purify the sons of Levi, and purge them as gold and silver."*
> (Malachi 3:2-3)

Living the Christian life is not a cakewalk. God does

not play games. He expects His people to be mature, upright, and straightforward—with a loving attitude. We are the clay, and He is the potter. *"But now, O Lord, thou art our father; we are the clay, and thou our potter; and we all are the work of thy hand"* (Isaiah 64:8). He will form us into His image the more we walk with Him. Salvation should be our main focus. To win the lost at any cost must be our priority, for Jesus is the greatest gift this world has ever received.

I have learned that we, the body of Christ, need the zeal and compassion that we received when we first believed in Him. We get out of focus and our vision becomes blurred when we are involved in schisms and divisions with fellow Christians. I have learned not to let so many things in the church bother me. Instead, I leave everything in God's hands. He knows what is best.

I have learned to involve my family more in the ministry, and to love and cherish my wife and children. It is easy to become a mechanical Christian, just going through the motions as time goes by. Fiery trials are allowed in order to renew our faith.

> *Beloved, think it not strange concerning the fiery trial which is to try you, as though some strange thing happened unto you:*
> *But rejoice, inasmuch as ye are partakers of Christ's sufferings; that, when his glory shall be revealed, ye may be glad also with exceeding joy.*
> (1 Peter 4:12-13)

It is important to give God thanks in all things. Be happy, smile always and be kind toward one another. Continue to plant the seeds of encouragement, hope and friendship. The Word cannot return void (Isaiah 55:11).

I have learned to take better care of my body, since it is the temple of the Holy Spirit (1 Corinthians 3:16). We are responsible for our actions—the way we eat, what we eat, how much rest we give our bodies. We should not take so much for granted. If we do not take good care of ourselves, we will not be around very long; or, if we are around, we will be limited in what we can do.

Keep in mind that we are the branches and Jesus is the vine (John 15:5). We can do nothing without Him.

Every branch in me that beareth not fruit he taketh away: and every branch that beareth fruit, he purgeth it, that it may bring forth more fruit.

I have learned that such purging is necessary to make us clean and able to contain more fruit.

"The gifts and calling of God are without repentance" (Romans 11:29). This means that God will not change His mind about using us for His service once He elects us. However, we can be preaching the Word every day, as I did, and still be missing something. It is more important to have a close relationship with Jesus than it is to evangelize the whole world. I found out that I cannot save the world by myself, but with God's leadership and anointing, my efforts are not fruitless. The Lord has saved and healed thousands of people through the ministry He has given me. Nothing that is done through me, however, can compare with what Jesus is about to do.

Our labor in His vineyard must come from the heart. Only then will our deeds be rewarded accordingly. Our deeds will be tried in the fire one day, and if they have really come from our hearts, they will not be consumed.

> *If any man's work abide which he hath*
> *built thereupon, he shall receive a reward.*
> *If any man's work shall be burned, he*
> *shall suffer loss: but he himself shall be saved;*
> *yet so as by fire.*
>
> (1 Corinthians 3:14-15)

There is a purpose for all things. *"All things work together for good to them that love God, to them who are the called according to his purpose"* (Romans 8:28). My kidney transplant ended up being good for me; it improved my relationship with my family, it improved my ministry, and, most importantly, it improved my relationship and love for God.

The Lord chastens those whom He loves: *"For whom the Lord loveth he chasteneth, and scourgeth every son whom he receiveth"* (Hebrews 12:6). We all need chastening and rebuking from time to time. It is good for us. It keeps pride out of our lives. God hates pride. Proverbs 8:13 says, *"The fear of the Lord is to hate evil: pride, and arrogancy, and the evil way, and the froward mouth, do I hate."* Arrogance hinders many ministers. Thank God for His love, for it keeps all of us in line with His perfect will.

Last but not least, I know that God will never leave us, through all the adversity, trials, troubles, and tribulations we face. And it is certain that we will face persecutions, according to 2 Timothy 3:12: *"All that will live godly in Christ Jesus shall suffer persecution."* God has proven to me that He is faithful and true (Revelation 3:14). He is *"the author and finisher of our faith"* (Hebrews 12:2). He is right here in the fire with us. *"Lo, I am with you always, even unto the end of the world"* (Matthew 28:20). Amen.

Testimonies of Others

*T*he following are testimonies that people have told me over the years of my ministry. I have included real names and addresses. My prayer is that you will see the power of God in each and every one of these true, miraculous stories.

⚡

I was involved in a head-on collision with another tractor-trailer. It took three hours to cut me out of the truck. I was all broken up. I lay in the University of Alabama Hospital for six weeks, bleeding internally. Doctors said I would not make it.

Brother Madison had preached in a revival in our church a year earlier, and I had seen a woman walk out of a wheelchair, so I knew Jesus was real. My wife called Brother Madison, and he came and anointed me with oil and laid hands on me. The bleeding stopped, and I left the hospital in a wheelchair about one and a half weeks later. I later walked out of the wheelchair, and now I am a walking miracle testimony for Jesus Christ.

—WILLIAM STOKES
Columbus, Mississippi

I had been deaf in my right ear for more than thirty years. During a revival in Birmingham, Alabama, Brother Madison prayed for Jesus to open it. Jesus healed my ear instantly, and I can hear out of my right ear now. I had several surgeries on this ear, but nothing worked except the healing power of God.

My daughter was born blind because she had no optical nerves. She was blind until she was four years old, but she can see now, thanks to Jesus. By the fifth grade, she could match her clothes. God healed her, and she is now a DJ at a Christian radio station and has recently married.

—LOIS HOWELL, *mother*
—APRIL BRASCOME, *daughter*
Birmingham, Alabama

I had been shot in the back in 1978, and the bullet was too close to my spine to operate. Doctors said I would have to live with it in my back and I would have constant pain. I was also on dialysis because of a bad kidney. I went to a revival where Brother Richard was preaching. He placed his hand where my kidney was and prayed for my back. He didn't know about the bullet, but he asked God to heal me of pain.

I had no more back pain after that night. A month later I had my back x-rayed, and the bullet had disappeared. The doctors were amazed, because there were no scars on my back. They knew I did not have any surgery. Jesus doesn't leave scars.

—CORY CAMERON
Wylam, Alabama

I had been diagnosed with cancer in my breast. I went to a revival in Opp, Alabama, and Brother Madison prayed for me. He told me to make the doctors take more x-rays, and nothing would be found. I went back the next day and had mammogram and ultrasound x-rays taken. The cancer had disappeared. I give God the glory and credit for healing me.

—MAC DESSIE KELLEY
Opp, Alabama

I was in an auto accident that put me into a coma three times. I remained in the hospital 142 days. I had twenty-eight surgeries and a $2 million hospital bill. Brother Madison and many other people of God prayed for me, and Jesus raised me up.

Brother Madison told his testimony to my mother. He also told her that Jesus was a healer and that He was going to heal me soon. Twenty-five days later, I came out of the hospital a walking miracle. Jesus also took care of the hospital bill. Praise God!

—BOBBY HILL
Cordova, Alabama

I was on $300 worth of heart medication per month. I had fallen away from God over fifty years ago. I heard Brother Madison's testimony on the radio, and I went to his revival in Adamsville, Alabama. He came over to me and put his hand on my chest, over my heart, and told me that God was going to give me a new heart. I asked Jesus to come back into my life, and I got a new heart in two ways. Jesus forgave me of my sins and healed my heart.

I went back to the doctor for my checkup and told him that I had quit taking the medicine. He examined me and found that I had a new heart. I had five heart bypasses several years before and could not even mow my lawn. But Jesus healed my heart, and the doctors saw the proof. Richard has a walk with Jesus and I know he lives what he preaches.

—EARNEST PERKINS
Birmingham, Alabama

I was blind in both eyes for many years. People had to lead me around. I asked my pastor to take me to one of Brother Madison's healing services. I knew that Jesus was the Healer, and I went to the service believing that I would receive my sight that night. While we were singing, I felt the Lord all over me. Instantly, my sight was opened and I could see.

—MOTHER GAINER
Panama City, Florida

I was shot four times by a deranged brother-in-law. I died in the hospital. I left my body and went to the graveyard in the spirit. There I saw where I would be buried. However, Jesus spoke to me and said, "Not yet, I am not finished with you." I woke up in Fayette County Hospital in Alabama, and the doctors were amazed. Jesus is real.

—MARIE BONNER UPTON,
Richard's grandmother
Oakman, Alabama

In September 1992, I was diagnosed with scoliosis at the Shriner's Hospital in South Carolina. Doctors said I must have surgery in order to get better. However, I was healed by Jesus in Brother Madison's service in October 1992. My spine is healed. I can bend, jump, and move about with no pain.

—CHERYLE GANT
Kimberly, Alabama

The sciatic nerve in my right leg was damaged in an automobile accident in August 1991. Brother Madison laid hands on me, and Jesus healed me. The numbness left my leg immediately, and I have no more pain.

—JEAN MYRICK
Birmingham, Alabama

I had been completely deaf in my left ear for twenty-five years due to nerve damage. Medical technology did not help. Hearing aids did not even work! But Brother Madison asked Jesus to open my ear, and immediately I could hear.

—WENDY COOK
Pinson, Alabama

As a truck driver, I had been a drunk for many years. I took pills every day. Then I heard Richard Madison tell about how Jesus had done so many things for him. I started believing that Jesus could do these things for me. And He has. I have not had a drink of alcohol since 1989. Jesus delivered my wife from alcohol, too, and He blesses us every day.

—JERRY & CHARCIE TILLMAN
Tarrant, Alabama

My brother Greg was shot between the eyes with a .25-caliber pistol in June 1992. He was in a coma for two months, and doctors sent him home with a breathing tube. They said he would never recover. Brother Madison came to our home and anointed Greg with oil and prayed the prayer of faith. Richard brought several people with him from the church at which he had been preaching. The power of God fell in Greg's room.

Brother Madison told us his testimony and showed us his scars. He said that Jesus was going to raise Greg up out of the coma. Several days later, Greg woke up from the coma. Now he is off the breathing machine and sitting up eating food. He is very alert and is getting stronger every day.

—BROTHER OF GREG SIMS
Piedmont, Alabama

I had a crooked spine and a hip that continually popped out of its socket. I had constant pain in my lower back and leg because of a pinched sciatic nerve. I was in pain even lying down. I could not do any housework, but I have been healed. Praise God! Brother Madison laid his hand on my head and prayed to Jesus, and immediately I was healed. I can bend, jump, run, even do housework with no pain.

—SUE GARBARD
Goodwater, Alabama

These are just a few of the thousands of healings, and miracles that my wife and I see and hear about. We give Jesus Christ the credit for all the souls saved and bodies healed. We preach the Gospel in order to see lives changed from sin to salvation, from bondage to freedom.

One January, Jesus spoke to me and told me that thousands of souls would be saved through my testimony in that year alone. I was already preaching on two different television stations in Alabama that go into eighty thousand homes. Then *The 700 Club* with Pat Robertson filmed and aired my testimony in July of that year, and has aired it several times since. *The 700 Club* was seen in over fifty million homes at the time. I knew then that this would be how God would save so many thousand of souls.

These are the last days, and God is pouring out His Spirit upon all flesh. He needs vessels through which He can work. I am just one of millions of vessels that God uses. Become a vessel for Jesus today. Ask Him now to forgive you and to come into your heart. He promised He would if you will ask Him to.

More Amazing Miracles

Here are a few more remarkable miracles that I witnessed. In 1988, I prayed for a deaf lady, a blind lady, and a man who could not speak. All of this happened in the same service. The blind lady received sight in her right eye instantly. I prayed for the deaf lady next, but she did not recieve her hearing.

I told her interpreter to bring her to the side. I wanted her to continue to thank Jesus for her hearing. The interpreter told her through sign language. I then began to pray for the man who could not speak. His wife told me he had a paralyzed tongue. I prayed for him twice. All of a sudden, the man began to make loud, strange sounds.

His wife started jumping and running, and I assumed he had never done this before. The interpreter with the deaf lady, told me she could hear the deaf man making sounds. Now this was a miracle. A deaf lady could hear a mute man making sounds, and a blind lady was watching it!

Another miracle happened when I went to a young man's home and prayed for him. He was diagnosed with cancer, and he was only twelve years old. He had lost his hair from the cancer treatments, and he had gotten worse. I told him he was healed, because Jesus took stripes across His back for our healing. I had Timothy to raise his hands, and thank Jesus for his healing. Two week later, the Lord impressed me to go to UAB hospital.

I went in the large lobby, wondering who I was there to see. Timothy's sister came up to me, and told me they had rushed Timothy into emergency surgery. She said tests had revealed that the cancer had doubled in Timothy's body. I told her this was impossible, because I knew Timothy was healed. She said they all knew that now. I asked her what she meant. She told me the doctors opened Tim up, and they could not find any cancer. She and I began to rejoice in the lobby.

I immediately went to Tim's room. When he saw me, he smiled real big, and he said, "Jesus really did heal me." The doctor walked in, and told Timothy that he had seen a miracle. The doctor said he had been asking God to show him that He was real. The doctor said, "I now believe there is a God." I said, "Yes, doctor, God is real, and his name is Jesus." The doctor then said he had called his wife and told her that they must begin to find out more about Jesus. Hallelujah!

Prayer to be Born Again

Father, I come to You in the name of Your Son, Jesus Christ, confessing with my mouth and believing in my heart that Jesus died for my sins and was raised to life on the third day. Father, You raised Jesus from the dead, and now He intercedes on my behalf. I am a sinner, and I have fallen short of the glory of God, but I repent of all my sins. I am now risen with Christ and I am born again.

I acknowledge that the precious blood of Jesus cleanses me from all sin, and that I am saved. I will testify that Jesus is Lord of lords and King of kings forever in my life. Thank You, Father, for writing my name in the Lamb's Book of Life. I am redeemed from the curse of the law and from sin. Since I have confessed with my mouth my faith in the Lord Jesus, and have believed in my heart that You raised Him from the dead, I now have eternal life. Amen.

Now tell everyone you see that Jesus is your Lord. Please find a church that believes in healings and miracles. Make sure the anointing is present.

Ask Jesus to fill you with the Holy Spirit. Also, get water baptized. Learn how to become the best disciple and read the Word of God. God bless you in all that you do for the Kingdom of God.

Your Brother in Christ,
Richard L. Madison

About the Author

Evangelist Richard L. Madison is an ordained full-time minister of the Gospel. He and his wife Paula, travel internationally with their healing and prophetic ministry. Richard speaks at various rallies, conventions, and revivals.

After his horrible car accident, Richard began to study under several pastors, and traveled with several evangelists. He then was instructed by the Lord to eat one meal a day for eighteen months. During this time, he learned about the anointing and how to flow in the gifts of the Spirit. Operation Healing Ministry began in 1987. Richard currently has a television ministry on Christian Television Network (CTN) now reaching half of the population of the world. CTN aires on Direct TV channel 376 and Dish Network channel 267. Rick Madison & Friends TV program is also on Glory Star, Sky Angel and many cable networks. Richard has been a guest on many TV networks including CBN (The 700 Club), Trinity Broadcasting Network, and Daystar Television Network. Richard Madison's ministry crosses all denominational lines. He and Paula minister wherever the Lord opens a door. Please feel free to contact Richard for revivals and campmeetings.

For information about books, CDs and DVDs contact him at (205) 622-5022 or visit www.rickmadison.org.

Cassette Tape/CD List

1. Walking Miracle Testimony
2. Receiving the Holy Ghost
3. The Names of God
4. Purposes of the Holy Ghost
5. The Fire, Voice and Obedience
6. Gifts of the Holy Spirit
7. Are You in the Fire?
8. What God is Doing Now
9. Daniel's 70th Week
10. Visions and Dreams
11. The Glory of God
12. The Bible Code
13. Healings and Miracles
14. Encounters of the Third Kind
15. Are You an Eagle Christian?
16. The Name of Jesus
17. Enoch and Elijah
18. Arise and Shine
19. Waiting on God
20. Overcoming Giants
21. Satan's Three Missing Stones
22. Why Jesus Died on a Cross?
23. Deserts, Caves and Mountains
24. Hebrew Alphabet I
25. Hebrew Alphabet II
26. Mystery of the Hours
27. Give the Woman What She Wants
28. What the Fig Tree Represents
29. Miracles I Have Seen
30. Mephibosheth and Jabez
31. What is Pentecost?
32. Jesus, the Suffering Messiah
33. Issues, Infirmities and Inabilities
34. We Must Die to Live
35. The Salt Covenant
36. Lion, Bear and Serpent
37. Eight Raptures in the Bible
38. Ashes of the Red Heifer
39. The Millenial Reign
40. Signs of Jesus' Return
41. God Warns His People First
42. The Prophecy of Jesus
43. God's Will for You
44. The Anointing
45. Revelation Knowledge
46. The Blood of Jesus
47. The Word of God
48. Hidden Manna
49. The Story of Job
50. A Still Small Voice
51. Power Comes After Prayer
52. The Five-Fold Ministry
53. Are You a Believer?
54. The Anointed Ones
55. The Peace of God
56. The Two Witnesses
57. World Events and US Presidents
58. The Rapture
59. Entertaining Angels
60. 7 Feasts of Israel
61. The Prayer Shawl
62. Wonders and Signs
63. All of Our Weapons
64. Days of Creation
65. Needs Met in the Glory
66. Intercessory Prayer
67. The Atonement
68. Walking by Faith
69. Satan, UFO's and Deception
70. Seeing in the Spirit

All tapes or CDs are $8.00 each OR 10 for $75.00 *(s/h included)*
Some messages available on DVD for $20.00 each or two for $30.00

The Anointing, Power & Gifts of God

by Richard L. Madison

Discover what it means to be born again. How to receive power through the infilling of the Holy Spirit. Learn how to hear the voice of God, and be led by His Spirit. The Anointing, Power and Gifts of God reveals the Biblical truths about salvation, sanctification, water baptism, and the baptism of the Holy Spirit. Learn about the gifts of the Spirit, how they operate, and how to flow in them.

Uncovered are seven purposes of the Holy Spirit, and what the Bible reveals is the evidence of being filled with the Holy Spirit. Learn about the fruit of the Spirit and how to apply them to your life. This is a biblical tool that helps explain the anointing of God, receiving revelation knowledge and how to have a personal relationship with Jesus Christ. There is a spiritual river flowing into all nations in these last days. Learn how to be a bold witness and be able to stand in these last and evil days. The perfect book to help you explain to others about the Holy Spirit. (110 pages)

—Price: $15.00

ISBN: 978-0-578-03736-3

End Time Prophecy Revealed

by Richard L. Madison

The most powerful and informative book on end-time events written in the past decade. Learn the secrets of the seven feasts of Israel, Daniel's 70 weeks, and the tribulation period. Discover the scripture passages that tell of the rapture of the Church. Will there be a catching away before, during, or after the tribulation? Learn what event begins the last seven years known as the tribulation period. Also includes recent information on how the United Nations, the Antichrist, and the banking industry will usher in the new world order. Startling evidence that Israel may begin animal sacrifices again. Discover the significance of the recent birth of the red heifer in Israel, and the development of the micro-chip implants. The unveiling of the two witnesses, the false prophet, and the next Middle East war. Includes the Jerusalem Covenant Document signed in 1993. A must for anyone interested in eschatology and future prophetic events. We are living in the last generation before the soon return of Jesus Christ. A great book to give your unsaved family and friends. It reveals that Jesus is coming soon.

ISBN: 978-0-578-04423-1 —Price: $15.00

Ministry DVDs

1. End Time Prophecy Vol. 1

This DVD covers the year 2012, prophetic cycles, signs of Jesus' return, US Presidents and Daniel's 70 weeks. The second message is titled Mystery of the Hours. It also covers the last days and how soon Jesus is coming back.

2. End Time Prophecy Vol. 2

The 1st message is The Lion, Bear, and the Serpent. The 2nd hour is Satan's Three Missing Stones. I promise this series will take you to another level.

3. End Time Prophecy Vol. 3

Two powerful messages. Prophetic Cycles includes information about solar and lunar eclipses in 2014 and 2015 known as tetrads. Nineteen year cycles from 1900 to 2012 are also revealed. The second message, Eight Raptures from Enoch to the White Throne Judgment, is a must study for end-time students.

4. Raised from the Dead

Richard shares his Miracle Testimony during a church service. The second message is titled Ashes of the Red Heifer and includes a powerful healing service.

5. Interview with Sid Roth and Marcus Lamb / Anointing and Funny Stories

DVD includes 4 TV programs - It's Supernatural with Sid Roth (actors re-enacting Rick's testimony). Rick also appears on Daystar with Marcus and Joni Lamb. The 3rd message is on the Anointing. Part 4 includes true funny stories that has occurred in Rick's services.

Ministry DVDs Continued

6. Faith Series

Richard preaches on how to use your faith, and how to receive from God. Includes miracles that Richard has seen such as coma patients waking up, the lame walking, and the blind receiving their sight. Learn how to pray for the sick and believe for the supernatural.

7. Entertaining Angels and Seeing in the Spirit

Two power packed messages that includes Richard sharing his encounters with real angels. Richard then shares on the lives of Elijah and Elisha and how they are a type of the end times. Richard also shares on how to see in the Spirit realm.

8. The Prayer Shawl and The Hebrew Alphabet

Richard shares on the Jewish Prayer Shawl while wearing one. A great healing message from Numbers to Revelation. A woman touched the hem of Jesus' garment and was healed. The second message parallels the 22 Hebrew letters with the 22 mysteries in the New Testament.

9. Overcoming Giants and Receiving Revelation Knowledge

Richard shares on the 5 giants King David killed, where they came from, and the meaning of their names. He also compares the lives of David, Jesus and the body of Christ and how we overcome the enemy. The Second hour includes how we can receive and retain revelation, wisdom, and knowledge. Richard shares how to hear from God for direction and instruction.

Ministry DVDs Continued

10. Eagle Christians and What's in a Name?

These are two great messages that will teach you the value of becoming an intercessor, reaching goals and finding your purpose. The second hour reveals God's covenants through the revelation of several Biblical names.

11. Financial Opportunities with Gold and Silver

This two and a half hour DVD is an interview Richard had with Terry Sacka – a leading financial adviser in the market of gold and silver. Sound advice with a Biblical perspective will prepare you for the future both economically and spiritually.

12. Laughter Doeth Good Like a Medicine

This is a great DVD that will keep you in stitches as Richard describes real events that have happened in his meetings or in hospital visits. Free with any other DVD order.

All DVDs are 2 hours in length and
are $20.00 each (s/h included)
Call (205) 622-5022 to order
or visit www.rickmadison.org
DVD specials available on website.

Watch Rick Madison & Friends
on the
Christian Television Network

Direct TV Channel 376
Dish Network Channel 267
or online at www.ctnonline.com.